Faith To Obey God

Kevin B. Brewer

Copyright © 2017 by Kevin B. Brewer

All rights reserved
Rejoice Essential Publishing
P.O. BOX 85
Bennettsville, SC 29512
www.republishing.org

All rights reserved. No part of this book may be used or reproduced by any means, graphic, electronic, or mechanical, including photocopying, recording, taping or by any information storage retrieval system without the written permission of the publisher except in the case of brief quotations embodied in critical articles and reviews.

Unless otherwise indicated, Scripture is taken from the King James Version.

Visit the author's website at www.fitwcc.org

Faith To Obey God/ Kevin B. Brewer

ISBN-10: 1-946756-11-3
ISBN-13: 978-1-946756-11-4

Library of Congress Control Number: 2017947880

DEDICATION PAGE

To Mom! Gertrude V. Brewer (June 14, 1929 – May 24, 2017)

Contents

Acknowledgements..viii

Foreword...x

Introduction..1

We Must Know The Voice Of God For Ourselves.......................7

We Must Know Our Specific Assignment From God................32

We Must Be Ourselves While Learning From Others.............40

We Must Be A Finisher, Not Just A Starter............................51

We Must Know Our Position As A Believer.............................62

We Must Not Be Concerned About Our Personal Reputation......73

We Must Know To Trust God Beyond Our Natural Understanding(s)..93

Conclusion...114

Table 1/Annex A...119

Table 2/Annex B...121

Index..135

ACKNOWLEDGEMENTS

To God our Saviour, by the Lord Jesus Christ, and the Holy Spirit by which I am empowered to generate this manuscript. To the entire staff at Rejoice Essential Publishing Company, and Prophetess Kimberly Hargraves, for all that they have done to make it possible for this manuscript to be published. Also, to Pastor Earl R. Brewer (Cleveland, OH), Bishop Willie S. Grant, Sr (James City, NC), Dr. Frederick S. Jones (Triangle, VA), and Apostle Frederick K. C. Price (Los Angeles, CA) all who pastored their own churches for "more than 30 years" each, and had monumental influence in my personal walk with God!

Foreword

Determined, charismatic, and wise is how I would describe Kevin B. Brewer. I can attest to his diligence to create the literary art called "Faith To Obey God." This work was cultivated over many years. However, it took tenacity and persistent to birth it out on paper. I was graced to witness this book come together in its final stages. It was so impressive that I offered him a publishing contract. He is truly an example of someone who is focused and will complete the given assignment. I can testify that as the weeks went by, he added more insight to perfect this book. He is very thorough, and he goes above and beyond in everything he does. The proof is in this book. He was my only client who ever provided Annexes in their manuscripts. As a CEO of an international Christian magazine "Rejoice Essential" and publishing company and author of over a dozen books, I would never foreword a book that I didn't believe in.

I recommend this book to use as an aid in the studying the bible. This book covers so many facets, from prophets to angels. There are many self-help books on the market, yet many of them fail to include real-life examples and the lessons gained from them. "Faith To Obey God" does both. So many people are afraid of the unknown. They have so many unanswered questions about life and their next steps in life. Kevin brings clarity to someone who may be facing these challenges. He does an amazing job of incorporating the Word of God into life examples that any reader can understand. As a full-time minister, I know about walking by faith. I wrote a book called, "Walking By Faith: A Daily Devotional." However, "Faith To Obey God" does an excellent job of describing that process.

I am glad that Kevin shares his wisdom inside this book because it caused me to look at things from a whole new perspective. I have read certain stories inside the bible numerous times, yet I never considered the faith it took for the biblical characters to accomplish what they did until I read through this book. Don't rush through this book. Read it and digest the words. Take notes and then seek God! You will discover that this book is full of spiritual meat. When you apply it to your life, you will be amazed at the transformation that will take place. As you do, get ready to receive many spiritual nuggets and impartation of knowledge.

Author Kimberly Hargraves
Rejoice Essential Publishing, LLC.
Founder and Chief Editor, Rejoice Essential Magazine.

CHAPTER ONE

Introduction

Many years ago, around the turn of the 21st century, I was invited to speak at an annual conference under the theme "Victorious Living for the 21st Century. After much personal prayer and fasting, God led me to speak on the subject of this book. Many of the things I was led to speak about are contained in this book, along with some updated wisdom keys God has provided me personally, in my life's journey of human experiences.

It should be obvious to most that as you live longer, you learn more about yourself, life, and who or what you believe in. If nothing else happens in your life, besides celebrating a birthday every year that you live - you learn. Even the bible says it this way in 1 Corinthians 13:11 (KJV) "When I was a child, I spake as a child, I understood as a child, I thought as a child: but when I became a man, I put away childish things."

Well, my personal journey in life with God has certainly allowed me to put away childish things, especially in my Faith to Obey God. A Faith to Obey God has to become an element of existence for daily living, that goes beyond natural comfort, and/or provisions. To Obey God has to become an everyday priority for one's personal life, and not a "just on Sunday" occurrence!

Many people have attempted to be faithful to God, in their attendance to a weekly church service, but most of the rest of the week is about their personal desires from God, for what they feel they need as their priorities for them, Not HIM. This has resulted in many becoming associated with the term "Church Goer," rather than Christian. The Church Goers mentality is to go anywhere where "the service" meets their approval for personal taste. Many say a prayer, asking God for His guidance of where to go, but after they arrive, they NEVER ask God again, before they just leave to find another Church, that suits them better personally. I have always agreed with this saying, "If being in a garage does not make you a car, then being in a church does not make you a Christian!"

In the life of Abraham in the bible, he is tested more than once in his faith to obey God, after he was 75 years old. Most of us have come to believe that by the time we reach 75 years old, it's time for us to make sure our burial plans are intact! This was the very age, where it is recorded that God reveals himself to

Abraham, not just as God, but with a test to Obey HIM! Genesis 12:4 (KJV) "So Abram departed, as the Lord had spoken unto him; and Lot went with him: and Abram was seventy and five years old when he departed out of Haran."

One thing for sure, at that age, Abraham certainly should have put away childish things by now! Abraham's life teaches us that you never get to old, to have faith to obey God! Even in his final test of Obedience, in Faith to God (with Isaac), didn't happen until after having Isaac (at 100 years old).

Genesis 21:1-5 (KJV) "And the Lord visited Sarah as he had said, and the Lord did unto Sarah as he had spoken. 2 For Sarah conceived, and bare Abraham a son in his old age, at the set time of which God had spoken to him. 3 And Abraham called the name of his son that was born unto him, whom Sarah bare to him, Isaac. 4 And Abraham circumcised his son Isaac being eight days old, as God had commanded him. 5 And Abraham was an hundred years old when his son Isaac was born unto him."

The purpose of this book, is to help those whose desire in life, is to fulfill their God-given purpose for living. I know I've needed help, but our natural world has set a standard of accomplishments and approvals, that never quite complete it in GOD. I have found that striving after the world's standards of success, never filled the emptiness that only God could fill. Besides, in the world, they are constantly changing the rules, as the years go by (paying taxes is a perfect example!). In the world's approval of academic achievement and success, you need a High school diploma, then a post graduate degree, then another post graduate degree, then another post graduate degree, and all those degrees are not Free! So, by the time you got all your academic achievement finished, you were too long in school to have any experience in the work force, and also to educated to get employment for the level of your qualifications. However, you still have all these educational loan bills due! But, no one could afford to hire you, at the level of your educational status, and PAY YOU WHAT YOU WERE WORTH, so you ended up on the street, possibly eating from trash cans with maybe a Ph.D Degree Certificate hanging on your mom's wall in her house! Or you took a job working next to someone who got a GED, and your paycheck and theirs are the same. Or they maybe your BOSS!

This is where the Faith to Obey God becomes so critical to live by. One of the things that I have noticed, in my own personal bible reading, was that none of the MAJOR Named people in the bible, were ever required to have academic degrees, to be used by God; even to do the things that medical science still can't figure out (even with 21st century technology). The bible records that the fisherman Peter, one of the original 12 disciples/Apostles of Jesus Christ, walked on water-Twice! Nowhere in the bible does it ever say that he had an academic degree in any subject; but he had Faith to Obey God to believe that if Jesus told him to "come" (Concentrate On My Example), that he could get out of a boat, in a storm, and walk on water!

Matthew 14:22-33 (KJV) "And straightway Jesus constrained his disciples to get into a ship, and to go before him unto the

Faith To Obey God

other side, while he sent the multitudes away. 23 And when he had sent the multitudes away, he went up into a mountain apart to pray: and when the evening was come, he was there alone. 24 But the ship was now in the midst of the sea, tossed with waves: for the wind was contrary. 25 And in the fourth watch of the night Jesus went unto them, walking on the sea. 26 And when the disciples saw him walking on the sea, they were troubled, saying, It is a spirit; and they cried out for fear. 27 But straightway Jesus spake unto them, saying, Be of good cheer; it is I; be not afraid. 28 And Peter answered him and said, Lord, if it be thou, bid me come unto thee on the water. 29 And he said, Come. And when Peter was come down out of the ship, he walked on the water, to go to Jesus. 30 But when he saw the wind boisterous, he was afraid; and beginning to sink, he cried, saying, Lord, save me. 31 And immediately Jesus stretched forth his hand, and caught him, and said unto him, O thou of little faith, wherefore didst thou doubt? 32 And when they were come into the ship, the wind ceased. 33 Then they that were in the ship came and worshipped him, saying, Of a truth thou art the Son of God."

This has always made me wonder, why (if I'm in a storm on the water) would I ask Jesus of all things, to walk on water in a storm? Knowing me, I would have said, "Hey, can you stop this storm?" However, Peter did ask, and Peter walked on the water twice! First - when he left the boat to go to Jesus, Second, after he had sank, Jesus and Peter walked back to the boat together! I also noticed that the storm never stopped while they were walking on the water, it didn't cease until they were come into the boat! That tells me that God has empowered us to be water-walkers even in our storms in life. God does not wait to be with us when things are over, but even in the midst of our storms!

Notice that Jesus' rebuke to Peter in his sinking on the water was, "thou of little faith," he did not say THOU OF NO FAITH! Those eleven disciples that stayed in the boat, never became water walkers! Yes, Peter had some trouble walking on the water, but he is still the only other water walker, we read about other than Jesus! Peter's record is still, because of His Faith to obey God, in spite of his sinking on the water, he was the only one that got out the boat! That in itself is key to operating in your faith to obey God. You must be willing to get out of the boat of success in the natural world, and trade it in for "water walking" success in GOD!

CHAPTER TWO

We Must Know The Voice Of God For Ourselves

One of the keys to having the faith to Obey God is knowing the voice of God for yourself. There are some believers that question if they truly hear the voice of God. There are still others, who feel that they can't hear His voice and seek out others to help them hear.

To know God's voice for yourself, you must maintain an active growing personal relationship with Him. This fact can be seen in our everyday life. If you have daily contact with someone, you have no problem recognizing his or her voice.

Have you ever noticed small children on the playground? If a child cries for their mother, the mother can recognize her child's cry in a group of children. Why? It is because of the relationship that they share. Knowing the voice of God is like this. It is all about maintaining a personal relationship with Him.

Some believers hear the voice of God clearly, but don't like the message(s). They reason within themselves "surely God doesn't want me to do that?" We must realize that whatever God may tell us to do or say, may not be readily accepted at first. However, through the test of time, we will find the wisdom God has revealed to us.

Jesus faced this same dilemma with his disciples. His response is recorded in Matthew 10:27-28. "What I tell you in darkness, that speak ye in light: and what ye hear in the ear, that preach ye upon the housetops. And fear not them which kill the body but are not able to kill the soul: but rather fear him which is able to destroy both body and soul."

We are all at different levels when it comes to recognizing the voice of God. Isn't it interesting though, "our ability to recognize the voice of God is in direct proportion to the amount of time we spend with Him." In other words, the more time we spend in the presence of God, the more we are able to accurately recognize His voice! Illustrations of this at various levels can be found throughout the Word of God. Here are a few to consider.

Can you see where you find yourself, or relate to one of these the most?

ABRAHAM

In Genesis 12:1-4, we read about God's conversation with Abraham. How did Abraham hear God? "Now the Lord had said unto Abram, Get thee out of thy country, and from thy kindred, and from thy father's house, unto a land that I will shew thee: And I will make of thee a great nation, and I will bless thee, and make thy name great; and thou shalt be a blessing: And I will bless them that bless thee and curse him that curseth thee: and in thee shall all the families of the earth be blessed. So Abraham departed, as the Lord had spoken unto him: and Abram was seventy and five years old when he departed out of Haran."

Here we find that Abraham recognized the voice of God and went to perform what God had asked him to do. Abraham didn't let "all the message" affect his obedience to the voice of God. Is this an example of YOU? Do we hear from God, but what God says to us, is not what we wanted to hear? Let's look closer at the details of what God said to Abraham, when he spoke to him. He basically told Abraham to get away, or leave everything that was normal for him. His whole entire life's history, God asked him to get away from it (GIVE it Up)! Then, on top of that, God tells Abraham to go to a new place... but where? Can you image what that was like for Abraham to tell Sarai, his wife? "Hey

Sarai, Humm, I just heard a voice from heaven, tell me to move away from here, and go to a new place! But I don't know where it is yet?" Can't you hear Sarai saying "you heard a voice from Heaven, tell you to leave all this and go somewhere else, but you don't know where we are supposed to be going? RIGHT!" Can you imagine the faith not only of Abraham to just hear God, but also His faith in God, to tell others that he had heard from God? No one else heard God speaking to Abraham but Abe (himself)! Can you image what SARAI was thinking about her 75-year-old husband? "Humm, It's not that he wants to move, BUT HE DOESN'T KNOW WHERE TO? Really?" BUT the story says Abraham and all who were connected to him... followed this Voice of God (that only one person heard)! Talk about FAITH TO OBEY GOD!

Notice that Abraham was 75 years old when he heard from God? I mean talk about having purpose in life? God waited 75 years, then began his conversation with Abraham for the next 100 years. Genesis 25:7 (KJV)"And these are the days of the years of Abraham's life which he lived, an hundred threescore and fifteen years." (175) Doesn't that give us hope? If God got more out of Abraham after 75 years old, than he had before being 75, then being a senior citizen in God, has new meaning for the life of older people!

Although the bible doesn't specifically detail exactly how Abraham "knew it (internal or external)" was the voice of God, it does say specifically that it was God's voice that he heard because of Genesis 12:1 (KJV)

"Now the Lord had said unto Abram, Get thee out of thy country, and from thy kindred, and from thy father's house, unto a land that I will shew thee:" Let's consider one other point to hearing the voice of God, specifically in Abraham's case. To obey the voice of God, is to obey it correctly when you hear Him!

Abraham was told in Gen 12:1:
Get out of thy Country
From thy kindred
From thy father's house
Unto a land I will show thee

However, in Gen 12:4 it shows that Abraham didn't obey the voice of God exactly, or correctly! Genesis 12:4 (KJV) So Abram departed, as the Lord had spoken unto him; and Lot went with him: and Abram was seventy and five years old when he departed out of Haran. This verse clearly states that Abraham didn't do what Gen 12:1 required. Abraham didn't follow the rules "From thy kindred" because Lot was his kindred, being the son of his deceased brother Haran. Genesis 11:27-28 (KJV) Now these are the generations of Terah: Terah begat Abram, Nahor, and Haran; and Haran begat Lot. 28 And Haran died before his father Terah in the land of his nativity, in Ur of the Chaldees.

Does this say something to us also? Do we long to hear God's voice, but fail to obey it exactly? Do we have a tendency to reason, "I know what God said, but that couldn't be what He really meant... Besides this is family! I can't leave them all by themselves, who is going to take care of them if I leave them all alone?"

We find here and later, in God's relationship with Abraham, that the family issues was the root cause of some of the uncomfortable struggles, Abraham experienced in his future. God becomes silent with Abraham after Gen 12:7 until Gen 13:14 when it is recorded that God doesn't speak to Abraham again until Lot is separated from him.

Genesis 13:14-15 (KJV) And the Lord said unto Abram, after that Lot was separated from him, Lift up now thine eyes, and look from the place where thou art northward, and southward, and eastward, and westward: For all the land which thou seest, to thee will I give it, and to thy seed for ever.

The strife between Abraham and Lot in Chapter 13 could have easily been avoided if Lot had not been there in the first place! Then there is the incident where Abraham does the rescue of Lot in Chapter 14.

Genesis 14:12-16 (KJV) And they took Lot, Abram's brother's son, who dwelt in Sodom, and his goods, and departed. 13 And there came one that had escaped, and told Abram the Hebrew; for he dwelt in the plain of Mamre the Amorite, brother of Eshcol, and brother of Aner: and these were confederate with Abram. 14 And when Abram heard that his brother was taken captive, he armed his trained servants, born in his own house, three hundred and eighteen, and pursued them unto Dan. 15 And he divided himself against them, he and his servants, by night, and smote them, and pursued them unto Hobah, which is on the left hand of Damascus. 16 And he brought back all the goods, and also brought again his brother Lot, and his goods, and the women also, and the people.

Last, but not least, is the famous story of Abraham bargaining with God over the lives in Sodom from 50 to 10. Genesis 18:22-33. Was Abraham really concerned for anyone more than his kindred family of LOT, who was there in Sodom (Gen 19:1)? Wasn't Abraham just trying to make sure that his Kindred family didn't get destroyed? So, was Abraham really thinking about the righteous as a whole, or was he being like us, trying to look out for family that God told us to get away from in the beginning, Gen 12:1?

Genesis 18:22-33 (KJV) And the men turned their faces from thence, and went toward Sodom: but Abraham stood yet before the Lord. 23 And Abraham drew near, and said, Wilt thou also destroy the righteous with the wicked? 24 Peradventure there be fifty righteous within the city: wilt thou also destroy and not spare the place for the fifty righteous that are therein? 25 That be far from thee to do after this manner, to slay the righteous with the wicked: and that the righteous should be as the wicked, that be far from thee: Shall not the Judge of all the earth do right? 26 And the Lord said, If I find in Sodom fifty righteous within the city, then I will spare all the place for their sakes. 27 And Abraham answered and said, Behold now, I have taken upon me to speak unto the Lord, which am but dust and ashes: 28 Peradventure there shall lack five of the fifty righteous: wilt thou destroy all the city for lack of five? And he said, If I find there forty and five, I will not destroy it. 29 And he spake unto him yet again, and said, Peradventure there shall be forty found there. And he said, I will not do it for forty's sake. 30 And he said unto him, Oh let not the Lord be angry, and I will speak: Peradventure there shall thirty be found there. And he said, I will not do it, if I find thirty there. 31 And he said, Behold now, I have taken upon me to speak unto the Lord: Peradventure there shall be twenty found there. And he said, I will not destroy it for twenty's sake. 32 And he said, Oh let not the Lord be angry, and I will speak yet but this once: Peradventure ten shall be found there. And he said, I will not destroy it for ten's sake. 33 And the Lord went his way, as soon as he had left communing with Abraham: and Abraham returned unto his place.

Just as a footnote of thought, look at the power of just 10 righteous folks! God would have saved two wicked cities from total destruction for just 10 righteous! Consider this also, although 4 were delivered out of the city, only 3 were saved! Lot's wife looked back and became a pillar of salt; because what was inside her from what she was leaving, was more powerful than her focus on what was before her?

Genesis 19:15 (KJV) "And when the morning arose, then the angels hastened Lot, saying, Arise, take thy wife, and thy two daughters, which are here; lest thou be consumed in the iniquity of the city."

Genesis 19:26 (KJV) But his wife looked back from behind him, and she became a pillar of salt.

Could this be us, God is leading us to a new beginning, but we keep letting the enemy call us back to remember our past, more than our present angelic deliverance!!? I call this a "Pillar of Salt" anointing, that leads to stifling results! One last thing before I leave the Abraham and Lot kindred connection. Lot became the father of the Moabites and the Ammonites.

Genesis 19:36-38 (KJV) Thus were both the daughters of Lot with child by their father. 37 And the firstborn bare a son, and called his name Moab: the same is the father of the Moabites unto this day. 38 And the younger, she also bare a son, and called his name Benammi: the same is the father of the children of Ammon unto this day.

These two families caused the children of Israel complications, throughout their 40 year wilderness journey to the promised land. Think about this, over 400 plus years of future trials could have been prevented, if Abraham had of just left Lot in Haran when God told him to leave his kindred. Does this speak to you? Do you hear God's voice, but you override it for Family? When I looked in the bible for Jesus's definition of family, it was recorded this way in Matt 12:46-50

Matthew 12:46-50 (KJV) While he yet talked to the people, behold, his mother and his brethren stood without, desiring to speak with him. 47 Then one said unto him, Behold, thy mother and thy brethren stand without, desiring to speak with thee. 48 But he answered and said unto him that told him, Who is my mother? and who are my brethren? 49 And he stretched forth his hand toward his disciples, and said, Behold my mother and my brethren! 50 For whosoever shall do the will of my Father which is in heaven, the same is my brother, and sister, and mother.

SAMUEL

Samuel had been around the man of God (Eli), working in the temple. Samuel heard a voice that seemed familiar to him as he slept. He went to Eli, because he thought it was Eli calling him.

I Samuel 3:1-10 (KJV)"And the child Samuel ministered unto the Lord before Eli. And the word of the Lord was precious in those days; there was no open vision. 2. And it came to pass at that time, when Eli was laid down in his place, and his eyes began to wax dim, that he could not see; 3.And ere the lamp of God went out in the temple of the Lord, where the ark of God was, and Samuel was laid down to sleep; 4. That the Lord called Samuel: and answered, Here am I. 5.And he ran to Eli and said, Here am I; for thou calledst me. And he said I called not; lie down again. And he went and lay down. 6. And the Lord called yet again, Samuel. And Samuel arose and went to eli, and said, Her am I: for thou didst call me. And he answered, I called not, my son: lie down again. 7. Now Samuel did not yet know the Lord, neither was the word of the Lord yet revealed to him. 8. And the Lord called Samuel again the third time. And he arose and went to Eli, and said, Here am I; for thou didst call me. And Eli perceived that the Lord had called the child. 9. Therefore Eli said unto Samuel, Go, lie down: and it shall be, if he call thee, that thou shalt say Speak Lord for thy servant heareth."

Samuel wasn't sure who was calling him. He was young and just didn't know. We can be like that young child Samuel ourselves, when we are young in our faith, and not sure about our ability to hear the voice of God. Samuel in his actions, teaches us a valuable lesson. He went to ELI for instructions on what to do. Sometimes we hear the voice of God and don't fully understand what to do. It is in these times that we can seek out our Spiritual authority person, who we have submitted our own selves too, for help in providing clarification.

Note: God is clear in that He would never allow his creation to be more accurate than Himself. We are not here to replace God, but to provide guidance for those seeking to develop their OWN personal relationship with God; on God's terms not ours! Look at this verse: 1 Samuel 3:10 (KJV) "And the Lord came, and stood, and called as at other times, Samuel, Samuel. Then Samuel answered, Speak; for thy servant heareth.

Another key we learn here is that God desires to be personally present in our personal areas (when dealing with us), and we learn that God uses repetitive measures that have become familiar to us (personally). Now in verses 11-15 we find that the Lord tells Samuel 5 clear things He plans to do, using the words "I Will," and "I have Sworn."

1 Samuel 3:11-15 (KJV) And the Lord said to Samuel, Behold, I will do a thing in Israel, at which both the ears of every one that heareth it shall tingle. 12 In that day I will perform against Eli all things which I have spoken concerning his house: when I begin, I will also make an end. 13 For I have told him that I will judge his house for ever for the iniquity which he knoweth; because his sons made themselves vile, and he restrained them not. 14 And therefore I have sworn unto the house of Eli, that the iniquity of Eli's house shall not be purged with sacrifice nor offering for ever. 15 And Samuel lay until the morning, and opened the doors of the house of the Lord. And Samuel feared to shew Eli the vision.

One note of focus: what God says to Samuel that is somewhat cliche, to those of us familiar in some Penecostal circles; God says "I will do a thing." He does not say, "I will do a NEW thing!" Which leads me to believe that, the thing that God does will be of such caliber, it will be the talk of the town for several days!

The last key to hearing God's voice in Samuel's case is the fact that God choose his "rest time" to approach him, not his busy daytime full of many distractions. When Samuel approaches ELI for the first time, ELI tells him to go lie down again. That indicates to me that this was supposed to be the time when one rested from a productive day of serving duties.

1 Samuel 3:5 (KJV) And he ran unto Eli, and said, Here am I; for thou calledst me. And he said, I called not; lie down again.

And he went and lay down. This lets me know that God desires to be present in our lives when no one else is our priority... even ourselves!

JONAH

Jonah was a prophet of God. He was in the habit of hearing God's voice. For Jonah, the voice of God was familiar, but he didn't like the message. An account of this is found in Jonah 1:1-3. "Now the word of the Lord came unto Jonah the son of Amitai, saying, Arise, go to Nineveh, that great city, and cry against it; for their wickedness is come up before me. But Jonah rose up to flee unto Tarshish from the presence of the Lord and went down to Joppa;

Isn't it interesting to note that Jonah heard the message and he tried to run from the presence of God? How can you "really" run from the presence of God? Isn't God everywhere (Omnipresent)? Like Duh? Before we get too critical of Jonah, we need to look at ourselves as well. How many times has God spoken to us, and we don't like the message and we "think we can flee" from His presence? Humm, like if I don't do it, he won't bother me again about it... really?

I believe that Jonah had no real problem with what God wanted to do, except He just didn't want to be the one to do it! How often does God come to us with an assignment, and we answer back to him about having someone else we know, who we think is better qualified for that assignment than us? Like God didn't know ALL of that info, we are enlightening him on, BEFORE he came to us... Really? I think Jonah shows us more of ourselves, in response to God, on a regular basis. I believe God is talking to a lot more of us on a regular basis; it's not that he isn't talking, it is really that we are not cooperating like Jonah!

Through reading the short 4-chapter book of Jonah, it becomes apparent that Jonah was very clear on hearing from God on a regular basis, but he was more concerned about His personal agenda. After all that Jonah did, and went thru in Chapters 1 and 2, chapter 3:1-2 reads almost verbatim as chapter 1:1-2.

Jonah 3:1-2 (KJV) And the word of the Lord came unto Jonah the second time, saying, 2 Arise, go unto Nineveh, that great city, and preach unto it the preaching that I bid thee.

It's like God says, "Hey have you been through enough doing it your way, can we try this again?" Chapter 3:3 is Jonah's answer, and key to everything when it comes to having faith to obey God! Jonah 3:3 (KJV) So Jonah arose, and went unto Nineveh, according to the word of the Lord. Now Nineveh was an exceeding great city of three days' journey.

In all that Jonah had tried to do on his own, when he finally yielded to God, on God's term, God had allowed him to end up

Faith To Obey God

in close proximity to the place he had asked him to go to in the first place! WOW. I wonder how much stuff we could have saved ourselves from going through, if we just obey God in the first place? I have personally learned that doing things the way God has asked me too, in the first place, saves me from a lot of personal mess! Just because we hear God clearly, and DO what God has required of us, doesn't mean we get to control the results to our personal liking. Look at the end of chapter 3 and the beginning of Jonah chapter 4. Jonah tries to justify his previous actions, as to why he disobeyed God's voice. Then on top of that, he asked to die!

Jonah 3:10 - 4:3 (KJV) "And God saw their works, that they turned from their evil way; and God repented of the evil, that he had said that he would do unto them; and he did it not. 4:1 But it displeased Jonah exceedingly, and he was very angry. 2 And he prayed unto the Lord, and said, I pray thee, O Lord, was not this my saying, when I was yet in my country? Therefore I fled before unto Tarshish: for I knew that thou art a gracious God, and merciful, slow to anger, and of great kindness, and repentest thee of the evil. 3 Therefore now, O Lord, take, I beseech thee, my life from me; for it is better for me to die than to live."

Humm, really? God should listen to Jonah? Right! Like God should listen to us, when we won't even listen to HIM! Wait, Jonah says in the above verses that he knows all this about God's qualities, yet he wants God to Change HIS character traits to suit Jonah's will. DUH? When God is GRACIOUS, MERCIFUL, SLOW TO ANGER, OF GREAT KINDNESS, and REPENTEST Thee of EVIL... humm which one of those makes God a murderer to Kill Jonah? RIGHT! God is so wise in his handling of the emotional attitude of Jonah! I think this would be called a case CLASSIC! God speaks to Jonah to teach Him a universal lesson learned (LL) about Himself in verses 6-11.

Jonah 4:6-11 (KJV) And the Lord God prepared a gourd, and made it to come up over Jonah, that it might be a shadow over his head, to deliver him from his grief. So Jonah was exceeding glad of the gourd. 7 But God prepared a worm when the morning rose the next day, and it smote the gourd that it withered. 8 And it came to pass, when the sun did arise, that God prepared a vehement east wind; and the sun beat upon the head of Jonah, that he fainted, and wished in himself to die, and said, It is better for me to die than to live. 9 And God said to Jonah, Doest thou well to be angry for the gourd? And he said, I do well to be angry, even unto death. 10 Then said the Lord, Thou hast had pity on the gourd, for the which thou hast not laboured, neither madest it grow; which came up in a night, and perished in a night: 11 And should not I spare Nineveh, that great city, wherein are more than sixscore thousand persons that cannot discern between their right hand and their left hand; and also much cattle?

We learn so much about Jonah in these verses, and maybe something about ourselves also: 1.The hearing of God's voice, does not make us God (obtained all of God's wisdom). 2. Though God uses us in certain ways, does not mean that God can't be God without us. 3. There is so much around us, that we are not in charge of, in this life. 4. Why do we feel that WHAT we feel on the inside of us, should rule our outward outcome/circumstances? 5. Why can we have pity for stuff we can't control (trees, plants, wild animals, stars, galaxies), but no pity for those who are just like us (people)? 6. Be glad that God is NOT us! 7. Let God be God, and we be obedient to God! 8. Always live in the mindset that we are not God, that God knows what is best for everyone! 9. Just because we have endured some trials, does not mean that dying is the only way out... There is life after death! Lazarus (John 11:14-44) and Jesus both proved that! 10. Most things in life, when it comes to dealing with something we didn't create, needs to be left up to the original creator for maximum positive results!

GIDEON

Gideon was a farmer who became the fifth judge of Israel. He heard the voice of God and questioned God's message. He was looking at his circumstances instead of listening to the voice of God. This account is found in Judges 6:14 -15. "And the Lord looked upon him, and said, Go in this thy might, and thou shalt save Israel from the hand of the Midianites: have not I sent thee? And he said unto him, Oh my Lord, wherewith shall I save Israel? Behold, my family is poor in Manasseh, and I am the least in my father's house."

Gideon also wanted reassurances from God every step of the way. This can be seen in Judges 6:36-40. Gideon is asking for a sign before he proceeded to do what God asked him to do. Have we ever done that? Got the T-shirt myself!

Judges 6:36-40 (KJV) And Gideon said unto God, If thou wilt save Israel by mine hand, as thou hast said, 37 Behold, I will put a fleece of wool in the floor; and if the dew be on the fleece only, and it be dry upon all the earth beside, then shall I know that thou wilt save Israel by mine hand, as thou hast said. 38 And it was so: for he rose up early on the morrow, and thrust the fleece together, and wringed the dew out of the fleece, a bowl full of water. 39 And Gideon said unto God, Let not thine anger be hot against me, and I will speak but this once: let me prove, I pray thee, but this once with the fleece; let it now be dry only upon the fleece, and upon all the ground let there be dew. 40 And God did so that night: for it was dry upon the fleece only, and there was dew on all the ground.

How many times do we want to have the Gideon anointing test, in our personal lives, before we obey God? I mean, like the fact that God even approached us isn't enough, by itself! Really? Humm, like God didn't know what we could do on our own, and what we couldn't do on our own? However, what's more important is what God's knows that everyone else will find out about God, when they see what God does using us; who seems to be so inadequate in man's eye's. I personally think God likes to use the most unqualified (messy by man's standards) in the physical/flesh outside, to show how big of a heart toward God there is in us, on the inside. I believe God loves to hear the words "You see that, that has to be nobody but God to accomplish that!

Or something like this "that ain't nobody but God doing all of that!" God gets the full credit all the time!

In chapter 7 of Judges, we see that God speaks to Gideon again, concerning flushing out his army of warriors. This blows me away, since I am a prior military serviceman. When it comes to having enough warriors to help you fight, I was never taught to choose them like this! Let's look closely at the voice of God to Gideon in this area.

Judges 7:2-7 (KJV) And the Lord said unto Gideon, The people that are with thee are too many for me to give the Midianites into their hands, lest Israel vaunt themselves against me, saying, Mine own hand hath saved me. 3 Now therefore go to, proclaim in the ears of the people, saying, Whosoever is fearful and afraid, let him return and depart early from mount Gilead. And there returned of the people twenty and two thousand; and there remained ten thousand. 4 And the Lord said unto Gideon, The people are yet too many; bring them down unto the water, and I will try them for thee there: and it shall be, that of whom I say unto thee, This shall go with thee, the same shall go with thee; and of whomsoever I say unto thee, This shall not go with thee, the same shall not go. 5 So he brought down the people unto the water: and the Lord said unto Gideon, Every one that lappeth of the water with his tongue, as a dog lappeth, him shalt thou set by himself; likewise every one that boweth down upon his knees to drink. 6 And the number of them that lapped, putting their hand to their mouth, were three hundred men: but all the rest of the people bowed down upon their knees to drink water.

7 And the Lord said unto Gideon, By the three hundred men that lapped will I save you, and deliver the Midianites into thine hand: and let all the other people go every man unto his place.

Can't you hear Gideon thinking "Wait a minute! You want me to fight the Midianites with just 300 of the original 32,000 I had? No way! I know you did the fleece thing and all, but this doesn't make any kind of military sense for victory." Gideon was exactly right, it didn't make military sense, it made God Sense! God had already said what he didn't want in verse 2. Judges 7:2 (KJV) "And the Lord said unto Gideon, The people that are with thee are too many for me to give the Midianites into their hands, lest Israel vaunt themselves against me, saying, Mine own hand hath saved me."

Talk about God having some unorthodox military qualifications. No commander would ever think that they are supposed to win a battle, and they have already lost over 99% of their personnel, before the battle even started! Gideon had heard God's voice, and even followed God's orders, but you have to know, if this guy needed a fleece anointing to even get started, he must be really tripping by now? Was this an official OMG (Oh My GOD) moment? Hey, it gets better

Judges 7:9-25 (KJV) And it came to pass the same night, that the Lord said unto him, Arise, get thee down unto the host; for I have delivered it into thine hand. 10 But if thou fear to go down, go thou with Phurah thy servant down to the host: 11 And thou shalt hear what they say; and afterward shall thine hands be strengthened to go down unto the host. Then went he down with Phurah his servant unto the outside of the armed men that were in the host. 12 And the Midianites and the Amalekites and all the children of the east lay along in the valley like grasshoppers for multitude; and their camels were without number, as the sand by the sea side for multitude. 13 And when Gideon was come, behold, there was a man that told a dream unto his fellow, and said, Behold, I dreamed a dream, and, lo, a cake of barley bread tumbled into the host of Midian, and came unto a tent, and smote it that it fell, and overturned it, that the tent lay along. 14 And his fellow answered and said, This is nothing else save the sword of Gideon the son of Joash, a man of Israel: for into his hand hath God delivered Midian, and all the host. 15 And it was so, when Gideon heard the telling of the dream, and the interpretation thereof, that he worshipped, and returned into the host of Israel, and said, Arise; for the Lord hath delivered into your hand the host of Midian. 16 And he divided the three hundred men into three companies, and he put a trumpet in every man's hand, with empty pitchers, and lamps within the pitchers. 17 And he said unto them, Look on me, and do likewise: and, behold, when I come to the outside of the camp, it shall be that, as I do, so shall ye do. 18 When I blow with a trumpet, I and all that are with me, then blow ye the trumpets also on every side of all the camp, and say, The sword of the Lord, and of Gideon. 19 So Gideon, and the hundred men that were with him, came unto the outside of the camp in the beginning of the middle watch; and they had but newly set the watch: and they blew the trumpets, and brake the pitchers that were in their hands. 20 And the three companies blew the trumpets, and brake the pitchers, and held the lamps in their left hands, and the trumpets in their right hands to blow withal: and they cried, The sword of the Lord, and of Gideon. 21 And they stood every man in his place round about the camp: and all the host ran, and cried, and fled. 22 And the three hundred blew the trumpets, and the Lord set every man's sword against his fellow, even throughout all the host: and the host fled to Bethshittah in Zererath, and to the border of Abelmeholah, unto Tabbath. 23 And the men of Israel gathered themselves together out of Naphtali, and out of Asher, and out of all Manasseh, and pursued after the Midianites. 24 And Gideon sent messengers throughout all mount Ephraim, saying, Come down against the Midianites, and take before them the waters unto Bethbarah and Jordan. Then all the men of Ephraim gathered themselves together, and took the waters unto Bethbarah and Jordan. 25 And they took two princes of the Midianites, Oreb and Zeeb; and they slew Oreb upon the rock Oreb, and Zeeb they slew at the winepress of Zeeb, and pursued Midian, and brought the heads of Oreb and Zeeb to Gideon on the other side Jordan.

Gideon receives his finally word from the voice of God in verse 9. Judges 7:9 (KJV) And it came to pass the same night, that the Lord said unto him, Arise, get thee down unto the host; for I have delivered it into thine hand. Gideon get thee down unto the host: FOR I HAVE DELIVERED IT INTO THINE HAND!"

What a final word from God, it's done and on my terms. Gideon says one last important key to his own men before they all go forth to battle. In verse 17 he says, look on me and do likewise. Those are some of the most powerful words in leadership everywhere. "Don't be me, be you, but do as I do." As a leader he says, I'm in this same thing with you! I'm not asking you to risk anything that I'm not personally risking myself. I got a word from God, and you have God's words from me! The fight is already ours. God just wants us to stand up and stand still for him!" God's going to show out, we just need to show up! Amen!!!!

MOSES

Moses was the deliverer of the children of Israel from their bondage in Egypt. He, like Gideon, heard the voice of God and began to look at his personal circumstances instead of operating in Faith to Obey God. This is seen in Exodus 3:10. "Come now therefore, and I will send thee unto Pharaoh, that thou mayest bring forth the children of Israel out of Egypt? And Moses said unto God, Who am I that I should go unto Pharaoh, and that I should bring forth the children of Israel out of Egypt?"

Here we have God telling Moses, at 80 years old (Exodus 7:7), you are to go back to the place you came from, and revisit your past; in order to do my will! Wow, do you want God to tell you that? I know I don't! Go back to the places and people that were trying to kill you, but you know their customs and procedures, because I let them raise you. The number 40 seems to have special meaning with Moses: 1. It is believed that Moses spent his first forty years growing up in Egypt. 2. It is believed that his second forty years was spent in the land of Midian 3. His last 40 years in the wilderness with the children of Israel. 4. He also spent 40 days on mount Sinai with God-no food or water - while with Israel in the wilderness (Exodus 24:15-18/Acts 7:23-30).

There is an interesting point about knowing the voice of God that is illustrated by Gideon and Moses. When we "personally" hear the voice of God, we need to take GOD at His word. We need to move out, follow His instructions and don't offer "our" excuses! Humm, like God didn't already know our situation before he spoke to us? Faith to Obey God is born when we hear God's voice, recognize it, and move out (obey-action) without excuses. In order to know God's voice for yourself, you must realize that whatever God has told you to say or do, will not be open arms accepted, by yourself or others. Isa 55:8-9 verifies that God operates on levels that are not common to us.

Isaiah 55:8-9 (KJV) 8 For my thoughts are not your thoughts, neither are your ways my ways, saith the Lord. 9 For as the heavens are higher than the earth, so are my ways higher than your ways, and my thoughts than your thoughts.

This means that in the wisdom of God, in the final results of our obedience, it will not be obvious at first, but must be revealed through our faith to obey, not just say! Knowing about God, is NOT the same as obeying God! The book of James says it like this in chapter 1:22 (KJV) "But be ye doers of the word, and not hearers only, deceiving your own selves."

Abraham, Samuel, Jonah, Gideon, and Moses teaches us the different levels it takes, to go from just hearing the voice of God to doing the will of God (from having heard HIS voice). Each one of those people teach us that God is very personable. He didn't approach all the same, and he never asked any of them to repeat what he had the others do! That is key! God is awesome enough to be original for each one he speaks to. God doesn't have to duplicate anything, or any assignment! His voice TO me will always be His voice FOR me!

CHAPTER THREE

We Must Know Our Specific Assignment From God

When we know the voice of God for ourselves, we will also know our specific assignment too! We cannot do someone else's assignment and be successful at it, without failing in our own.

Consider this example: I ask my oldest son to wash the dishes in the kitchen sink, before I return home, and ask my youngest son to mop the kitchen floor, when his brother is done. When I return home, and find that the floor has been mopped, the windows washed, the refrigerator defrosted, and the entire carpets vacuum; but the dishes are still dirty in the sink. Will it matter to me that my oldest son was the one that did all those wonderful things, or will it matter that he did not DO what I asked of him?

A lot of times we do a lot of other things that keep us busy and are very good things to get done; BUT... the specific assignment that was given to us, has still yet to be accomplished by us. We do "what others are doing," but NOT what God specifically assigned to us! In the bible, in the book of Acts 5:17-19 it tells of the story of the apostles being liberated from prison, but for a specific reason..."speak in the temple, to the people, all the words of this life."

Acts 5:17-21 (KJV) Then the high priest rose up, and all they that were with him, (which is the sect of the Saducees,) and were filled with indignation, 18 And laid their hands on the apostles, and put them in the common prison. 19 But the angel of the Lord by night opened the prison doors, and brought them forth, and said, 20 Go, stand and speak in the temple to the people all the words of this life. 21 And when they heard that, they entered into the temple early in the morning, and taught.

They (the Apostles) had NOT been liberated from prison to do their own thing, but there was a specific reason for them being set free... a specific assignment! Jesus makes a specific warning in the Bible about saying one thing, but not doing the right thing.

Matthew 7:20-23 (KJV) Wherefore by their fruits ye shall know them. 21 Not every one that saith unto me, Lord, Lord, shall enter into the kingdom of heaven; but he that doeth the will of my Father which is in heaven. 22 Many will say to me in that day, Lord, Lord, have we not prophesied in thy name? and in thy name have cast out devils? and in thy name done many wonderful works? 23 And then will I profess unto them, I never knew you: depart from me, ye that work iniquity.

When we follow God's word for our lives, we must rest in the fact that it is on God to make Himself look good, not us. Ex: If I need something in my life to help me improve my image, I can do it myself, or call upon someone else to help me. However, if I choose to use someone else, then it is incumbent upon me to empower them, with the proper resources, in order for them to be truly successful in acquiring what I asked them to do, ultimately improving my own image.

So it is with God. Look at Matt 5:17-20 again, if God wanted them to stand in the Temple to speak to the people, then he had to first open the doors to their prison. But pay attention to the order of events, the doors were already opened for them, before God asked them to do something. When we do our specific assignment, God has already opened the doors for us to have success on His terms. It's not that He will open the door, but that he has already done so!

Knowing ones' specific assignment also involves a "timing" element. What I mean by that is this, doing what God asked me to do, is specifically connected to a timing sequence in my life. Look at Jesus's life, he was here for one major assignment (go to calvary), but it could not be done until Jesus had reached a certain timing (age) in his life. He was born 30 years before he was ready to complete his specific assignment (Luke 3:21-23). The assignment was always the same from birth to the cross, but the timing of when it took place, was also specific.

I submit to you that timing is just as important as the specific assignment. Even though you may be called to accomplish a specific task, the timing of that accomplishment is just as important, as the doing of the task. Many of us want to know what to do, but I submit to you that knowing WHEN to do it, is just as important for successful results to occur! Hearing God's voice is important. Knowing what specific task God has assigned is important; but knowing when to accomplish it, is just as important!

Don't just seek God for what to do, seek him for when to do it also! Think of it this way, when I'm born into this world, I have the potential, all things operating properly, to one day drive a vehicle. However, though I have the potential to drive, I must respect the timing of WHEN I qualify to drive! Many of us attempt to accomplish things in God, before the proper element of TIME is in place.

My favorite biblical example of this point, is the deliverance of the children of Israel from Egypt. They were never delivered by Moses because THEY wanted to be delivered, they were delivered from Egypt because of a promise God had made to Abraham some 400 years earlier. Look at this passage in Genesis chapter 15.

Genesis 15:12-14 (KJV) And when the sun was going down, a deep sleep fell upon Abram; and, lo, a horror of great darkness fell upon him. 13 And he said unto Abram, Know of a surety that thy seed shall be a stranger in a land that is not theirs, and shall serve them; and they shall afflict them four hundred years; 14 And also that nation, whom they shall serve, will I judge: and afterward shall they come out with great substance.

Here God sets the specific timing of the specific assignment of Moses, with Abraham 400 years before it would happen. The bible also records that it took place 430 years to the day. Look at Exodus chapter 12. Exodus 12:40-41 (KJV) Now the sojourning of the children of Israel, who dwelt in Egypt, was four hundred and thirty years. 41 And it came to pass at the end of the four hundred and thirty years, even the selfsame day it came to pass, that all the hosts of the Lord went out from the land of Egypt.

Another factor here is that as much as the children of Israel cried and mourned about their conditions, there was God's perfect timing involved in the specific assignment of their deliverance. Four hundred years was key to the timing of Abraham's seed being delivered by Moses, because God had already promised Abraham.

Note also that when Abraham left from Egypt in Genesis chapter 13, he left abundantly rich. So, when his descendants left Egypt, four hundred years later they left rich as well. It was generational blessings being passed down. Compare these scriptures:

Genesis 13:1-2 (KJV) And Abram went up out of Egypt, he, and his wife, and all that he had, and Lot with him, into the south. 2 And Abram was very rich in cattle, in silver, and in gold.

Exodus 12:35-36 (KJV) And the children of Israel did according to the word of Moses; and they borrowed of the Egyptians jewels of silver, and jewels of gold, and raiment: 36 And the Lord gave the people favour in the sight of the Egyptians, so that they lent unto them such things as they required. And they spoiled the Egyptians.

Do you remember what God had told Abraham originally four hundred years prior? let's read it again. Genesis 15:14 (KJV) 14 And also that nation, whom they shall serve, will I judge: and afterward shall they come out with great substance. Here we see that the principle of knowing your specific assignment, is also tied to knowing the specific timing to the success of that assignment also. Moses could have never delivered the children of Israel out of Egypt, if Joseph had never brought Jacob (Israel) into Egypt.

Genesis 46:26-27 (KJV) All the souls that came with Jacob into Egypt, which came out of his loins, besides Jacob's sons' wives, all the souls were threescore and six; 27 And the sons of Joseph, which were born him in Egypt, were two souls: all the souls of the house of Jacob, which came into Egypt, were threescore and ten (70).

Seventy souls originally came into Egypt with Jacob and Joseph, and 430 years later from Abraham, over 600,000 plus came out. Exodus 12:37-38 (KJV) And the children of Israel journeyed from Rameses to Succoth, about six hundred thousand on foot that were men, beside children. 38 And a mixed multitude went up also with them; and flocks, and herds, even very much cattle.

Here is an interesting note. Over 600,000 originally came out of Egypt, on that great deliverance day known as the night of passover. However, some 40 years later, only two of the original 600,000 (20 years old and upward), mentioned to have made it to the promised land-Joshua and Caleb! (Not even Moses).

Numbers 14:26-38 (KJV) And the Lord spake unto Moses and unto Aaron, saying, 27 How long shall I bear with this evil congregation, which murmur against me? I have heard the murmurings of the children of Israel, which they murmur against me. 28 Say unto them, As truly as I live, saith the Lord, as ye have spoken in mine ears, so will I do to you: 29 Your carcases shall fall in this wilderness; and all that were numbered of you, according to your whole number, from twenty years old and upward, which have murmured against me, 30 Doubtless ye shall not come into the land, concerning which I sware to make you dwell therein, save Caleb the son of Jephunneh, and Joshua the son of Nun. 31 But your little ones, which ye said should be a prey, them will I bring in, and they shall know the land which ye have despised. 32 But as for you, your carcases, they shall fall in this wilderness. 33 And your children shall wander in the wilderness forty years, and bear your whoredoms, until your carcases be wasted in the wilderness. 34 After the number of the days in which ye searched the land, even forty days, each day for a year, shall ye bear your iniquities, even forty years, and ye shall know my breach of promise. 35 I the Lord have said, I will surely do it unto all this evil congregation, that are gathered together against me: in this wilderness they shall be consumed, and there they shall die. 36 And the men, which Moses sent to search the land, who returned, and made all the congregation to murmur against him, by bringing up a slander upon the land, 37 Even those men that did bring up the evil report upon the land, died by the plague before the Lord. 38 But Joshua the son of Nun, and Caleb the son of Jephunneh, which were of the men that went to search the land, lived still.

Let me say it one last time, we must know our specific assignment from God, but we must also know the specific timing too! I submit that Faith to Obey God must include God's timing, not just ours! Abraham, Jacob, Joseph, Moses, Joshua, and the apostles, all had specific assignments from God, but they also had specific timing sequences too!

CHAPTER FOUR

We Must Be Ourselves While Learning From Others

We need to be God approved, more than Man approved. 2 Timothy 2:15 (KJV) says "Study to shew thyself approved unto God, a workman that needeth not to be ashamed, rightly dividing the word of truth." We should have mentoring, not duplication. Many of us, in the 20th century, were ashamed of trusting God for ourselves, so it was a much easier faith fight to do what someone else was doing, rather than to stand-alone-with God, and do what had never been done before. It's the old saying that

"Chickens flock together, and Eagles fly alone" For the most part, Chickens die in the same place where they are born, yet Eagles soar above the challenge, to new heights not seen with common eyesight. And remember this, "Eagles have, from time to time, been considered endangered species, whereas chickens never will!"

We need to ALWAYS understand that God knows what our limitations are, before He calls us. So, realize that whenever He calls us, to do something for/with Him; He had already planned to get involved in it - with us! Look at 2 Corinthians 6:1 (KJV) "We then, as workers together with him, beseech you also that ye receive not the grace of God in vain."

The apostle Paul writes to the church at Corinth, that he was in assignment with God, by God's grace upon his life, to not be a vain tasking for them to receive his words. We must also understand that when it is finished (whatever we are to accomplish), the only words that are supposed to be heard by all the on lookers are: "Look at God!" The Story of Joseph has been called from the "Pit to the Place." Yet, the real issue was, that Joseph was "called" to be different from all the rest, from the very beginning. He could never fit in because he was never suppose to!

Genesis 37:23-24 (KJV) And it came to pass, when Joseph was come unto his brethren, that they stript Joseph out of his coat, his coat of many colours that was on him; 24 And they took him, and cast him into a pit: and the pit was empty, there was no water in it. Then two chapters later it reads

Genesis 39:1-4 (KJV) And Joseph was brought down to Egypt; and Potiphar, an officer of Pharaoh, captain of the guard, an Egyptian, bought him of the hands of the Ishmaelites, which had brought him down thither. 2 And the Lord was with Joseph, and he was a prosperous man; and he was in the house of his master the Egyptian. 3 And his master saw that the Lord was with him, and that the Lord made all that he did to prosper in his hand. 4 And Joseph found grace in his sight, and he served him: and he made him overseer over his house, and all that he had he put into his hand.

However, he still doesn't get to fit in, starting in verse 17

Genesis 39:17-23 (KJV) And she spake unto him according to these words, saying, The Hebrew servant, which thou hast brought unto us, came in unto me to mock me: 18 And it came to pass, as I lifted up my voice and cried, that he left his garment with me, and fled out. 19 And it came to pass, when his master heard the words of his wife, which she spake unto him, saying, After this manner did thy servant to me; that his wrath was kindled. 20 And Joseph's master took him, and put him into the prison, a place where the king's prisoners were bound: and he was there in the prison. 21 But the Lord was with Joseph, and shewed him mercy, and gave him favour in the sight of the keeper of the prison. 22 And the keeper of the prison committed to Joseph's hand all the prisoners that were in the prison; and whatsoever they did there, he was the doer of it. 23 The keeper of the prison looked not to anything that was under his hand; because the Lord was with him, and that which he did, the Lord made it to prosper.

Everywhere Joseph ended up, he stood out from all the rest, from family to employment, yet he was learning about others from every encounter! Could God be educating him for his future destiny in every encounter?

Finally, in Genesis 41:37-41 (KJV) And the thing was good in the eyes of Pharaoh, and in the eyes of all his servants. 38 And Pharaoh said unto his servants, Can we find such a one as this is, a man in whom the Spirit of God is? 39 And Pharaoh said unto Joseph, Forasmuch as God hath shewed thee all this, there is none so discreet and wise as thou art: 40 Thou shalt be over my house, and according unto thy word shall all my people be ruled: only in the throne will I be greater than thou. 41 And Pharaoh said unto Joseph, See, I have set thee over all the land of Egypt.

Genesis 41:44 (KJV) And Pharaoh said unto Joseph, I am Pharaoh, and without thee shall no man lift up his hand or foot in all the land of Egypt." In the last century, we as a people wasted a lot of time trying to change ourselves to fit the approval of man; when that act in itself is an indictment against God, and His creative genius in making us all unique.

It's all right to imitate, but if God wanted cloning, He can do it without our help. Besides, where God is concern, to make copies would have been a lot easier than making an original free-willed being every time. Think about this, even twins are supposed to have their own separate finger prints! The individuality that each one of us has, brings out the greatness of the super intelligence of God; as the Creator!

If learning from others is critical to the proper advancement in life, why not learn from others on how to be ourselves in God? When we read about all those who had "specific assignments" from God in the bible, we find that none of them had the SAME exact assignment. Of all the 12 disciples that Jesus hand picked, during his physical journey to Calvary's cross, none of them wrote more in the Bible than Paul! Paul is never considered as being one of the original 12, but he wrote more in the bible than all the other Apostles. The apostle Paul of the Bible, is a prime example of being ourselves while learning from others.

Each one of us has been destined to accomplish something special and specific, to the enhancement of the Kingdom of God while in this dimension. God who created us unique to ourselves, need not make us a second to the original, but have us remain the original that God made us! Even with mentoring, the mentor is not trying to make you be a copy of themselves, but the best YOU can become of YOU, with their wisdom and help.

One of the best stories in the Bible that illustrates this principle is the Elijah/Elisha team. Elijah is told by God to call Elisha as his successor. 1 Kings 19:15-16 (KJV) And the Lord said unto him, Go, return on thy way to the wilderness of Damascus: and when thou comest, anoint Hazael to be king over Syria: 16 And Jehu the son of Nimshi shalt thou anoint to be king over Israel: and Elisha the son of Shaphat of Abelmeholah shalt thou anoint to be prophet in thy room.

One of the reasons I believe that Elisha was chosen in the first place, was because of Elijah's perception of life's current situation; that he was the only one serving God, and that his life was being sought for the killing by people! Have you ever had the wrong perception of what was really going on in life, and rather than Have faith in God, you believed the publicity of man over the promises; or past victories you have had in God? Besides, when you are having a personal conversation with God, "fear" is not the vehicle you need to be riding in, when conversating with the God of the Universe! Telling God what people are talking about doing to you, is not high on the GOD list! Telling God who He is to YOU, in spite of people, is so much better!

Let's Read 1 Kings 19:9-14 (KJV) And he came thither unto a cave, and lodged there; and, behold, the word of the Lord came to him, and he said unto him, What doest thou here, Elijah? 10 And he said, I have been very jealous for the Lord God of hosts: for the children of Israel have forsaken thy covenant, thrown down thine altars, and slain thy prophets with the sword; and I, even I only, am left; and they seek my life, to take it away. 11

And he said, Go forth, and stand upon the mount before the Lord. And, behold, the Lord passed by, and a great and strong wind rent the mountains, and brake in pieces the rocks before the Lord; but the Lord was not in the wind: and after the wind an earthquake; but the Lord was not in the earthquake: 12 And after the earthquake a fire; but the Lord was not in the fire: and after the fire a still small voice. 13 And it was so, when Elijah heard it, that he wrapped his face in his mantle, and went out, and stood in the entering in of the cave. And, behold, there came a voice unto him, and said, What doest thou here, Elijah? 14 And he said, I have been very jealous for the Lord God of hosts: because the children of Israel have forsaken thy covenant, thrown down thine altars, and slain thy prophets with the sword; and I, even I only, am left; and they seek my life, to take it away.

The Bible points out things in these scriptures that I believe are important to remember: 2 Timothy 1:7 (KJV) For God hath not given us the spirit of fear; but of power, and of love, and of a sound mind. And 1 John 4:18 (KJV) There is no fear in love; but perfect love casteth out fear: because fear hath torment. He that feareth is not made perfect in love. And 1 John 5:4 (KJV) For whatsoever is born of God overcometh the world: and this is the victory that overcometh the world, even our faith.

The enemy is empowered by our fear, and God is influenced by our Faith! You are never in both (Faith and Fear) at the same time, because they are opposites to each other! You will either be operating in one, or the other! Let's now look closer at the Elijah/Elisha's famous exchange:

2 Kings 2:1-11 (KJV) And it came to pass, when the Lord would take up Elijah into heaven by a whirlwind, that Elijah went with Elisha from Gilgal. 2 And Elijah said unto Elisha, Tarry here, I pray thee; for the Lord hath sent me to Bethel. And Elisha said unto him, As the Lord liveth, and as thy soul liveth, I will not leave thee. So they went down to Bethel. 3 And the sons of the prophets that were at Bethel came forth to Elisha, and said unto him, Knowest thou that the Lord will take away thy master from thy head to day? And he said, Yea, I know it; hold ye your peace. 4 And Elijah said unto him, Elisha, tarry here, I pray thee; for the Lord hath sent me to Jericho. And he said, As the Lord liveth, and as thy soul liveth, I will not leave thee. So they came to Jericho. 5 And the sons of the prophets that were at Jericho came to Elisha, and said unto him, Knowest thou that the Lord will take away thy master from thy head to day? And he answered, Yea, I know it; hold ye your peace. 6 And Elijah said unto him, Tarry, I pray thee, here; for the Lord hath sent me to Jordan. And he said, As the Lord liveth, and as thy soul liveth, I will not leave thee. And they two went on. 7 And fifty men of the sons of the prophets went, and stood to view afar off: and they two stood by Jordan. 8 And Elijah took his mantle, and wrapped it together, and smote the waters, and they were divided hither and thither, so that they two went over on dry ground. 9 And it came to pass, when they were gone over, that Elijah said unto Elisha, Ask what I shall do for thee, before I be taken away from thee. And Elisha said, I pray thee, let a double portion of thy spirit be upon me. 10 And he said, Thou hast asked a hard thing: nevertheless, if thou see me when I am taken from thee, it shall

be so unto thee; but if not, it shall not be so. 11 And it came to pass, as they still went on, and talked, that, behold, there appeared a chariot of fire, and horses of fire, and parted them both asunder; and Elijah went up by a whirlwind into heaven.

In the passage above, it clearly states that Elijah departed into heaven by a WHIRLWIND, NOT A CHARIOT OF FIRE! It states it twice that the WHIRLWIND was the method of transportation for ELIJAH into Heaven!

In vs 9, it also states that Elisha didn't ask for Elijah's mantle, but for a Double portion of his SPIRIT! A mantle was something outside that man controls, both on or off of himself; whereas the spirit was a WITHIN mechanism for guidance and obedience. What I believe Elisha was saying to Elijah was, "Let me be able to obey God, as well as, I have seen you obey God! Knowing myself, I'm going to need double of what you had, in order to be as dedicated as I observed you be!" Elisha was asking for the God that was with Elijah, to be the same God that would be with him. Elisha was being (knowing) himself, while learning from others (Elijah)!

One of the first things that Elisha does to confirm that the God of Elijah, was with Him was to take the mantle that DIDNOT fall on Elisha, but fell from Elijah, and go to do with the fallen mantle, what he saw Elijah had used it for!

2 Kings 2:13-14 (KJV) He took up also the mantle of Elijah that fell from him, and went back, and stood by the bank of

Jordan; 14 And he took the mantle of Elijah that fell from him, and smote the waters, and said, Where is the Lord God of Elijah? and when he also had smitten the waters, they parted hither and thither: and Elisha went over.

Nowhere in that passage of Scripture does it say that the mantle fell ON Elisha! It says that he took it up, which makes me believe that it landed somewhere else, but NOT on Himself; if he had to take it up! It also never says that the mantle was now the Mantle of Elisha, even with Elijah gone, it keeps referring to it as "the mantle of Elijah."

The last thing that is key here, is that Elisha says a key phrase in his use of the mantle operation, Elisha says "Where is the Lord God of Elijah?! Elisha was being himself, while having learned from others!

It's important to note also that both Elijah (Jehovah is God), and Elisha (God is Salvation) did several acts of miracle power; but the Bible does record more of Elisha's works than Elijah's. The Bible records in 1 Kings 17 through 2 Kings 1:12 that Elijah had the Widow's oil, Dead child raised, Causes Rain, Causes fire to consume the sacrifice, and Causes fire to consume soldiers. However, from 2 Kings 2 through 6:23 it records the miracles of Elisha being Divides the Jordan, Purifies water, Increases widow's oil, Raises Shunamites son, Neutralizes poison, Multiplies bread, Heals Naaman of leprosy, Inflicts Gehazi with Leprosy, Cause axe handle to float, Reveals secret counsels, Opens servants eyes, Smites Syrians army with Blindness.

Now to be fair, we must remember that Elijah was not here as long as Elisha, because Elijah was taken up by a whirlwind, and Elisha did die! Interesting though, even as a dead man, Elisha's grave brought another man back to life, even though it didn't keep him alive!

Did you know this story was in the Bible? 2 Kings 13:20-21 (KJV) And Elisha died, and they buried him. And the bands of the Moabites invaded the land at the coming in of the year. 21 And it came to pass, as they were burying a man, that, behold, they spied a band of men; and they cast the man into the sepulchre of Elisha: and when the man was let down, and touched the bones of Elisha, he revived, and stood up on his feet.

Talk about being ourselves; Elisha's bones cause another dead man to revive and stand up! What would this world be like if everyone was a duplicate of Elisha, instead of their own original from God, when they died? Humm? Faith to Obey God is to believe that who God made you to be is enough for God to use you, just as He made you! Be all you can be (yourself) in God, not man!

CHAPTER FIVE

We Must Be A Finisher, Not Just A Starter

Ecclesiastes 7:8 (KJV) "Better is the end of a thing than the beginning thereof: and the patient in spirit is better than the proud in spirit."

Of course that scripture says a lot of things on several levels, but I have coined the following saying from the first part of it "It's not how you start out, but how you end (finish) up!" Luke 2:6-7 (KJV) And so it was, that, while they were there, the days were accomplished that she should be delivered. 7 And she brought forth her firstborn son, and wrapped him in swaddling clothes, and laid him in a manger; because there was no room for them in the inn. Did you notice that vs 7 says "her firstborn, NOT her "ONLY" BORN?" Humm, Mary wasn't finished with having children after Jesus had been born? That was good news for her husband Joseph!

Luke 23:50 - 24:6 (KJV) "And, behold, there was a man named Joseph, a counsellor; and he was a good man, and a just: 51 (The same had not consented to the counsel and deed of them;) he was of Arimathaea, a city of the Jews: who also himself waited for the kingdom of God. 52 This man went unto Pilate, and begged the body of Jesus. 53 And he took it down, and wrapped it in linen, and laid it in a sepulchre that was hewn in stone, wherein never man before was laid. 54 And that day was the preparation, and the sabbath drew on. 55 And the women also, which came with him from Galilee, followed after, and beheld the sepulchre, and how his body was laid. 56 And they returned, and prepared spices and ointments; and rested the sabbath day according to the commandment. 1 Now upon the first day of the week, very early in the morning, they came unto the sepulchre, bringing the spices which they had prepared, and certain others with them. 2 And they found the stone rolled away from the sepulchre. 3 And they entered in, and found not the body of the Lord Jesus. 4 And it came to pass, as they were much perplexed thereabout, behold, two men stood by them in shining garments: 5 And as they were afraid, and bowed down their faces to the earth, they said unto them, Why seek ye the living among the dead? 6 He is not here, but is risen: remember how he spake unto you when he was yet in Galilee,"

Jesus started out in a manger, but finished up on a cross for all mankind! Then they put him in a tomb, but three days later, that same tomb became empty by his resurrection! I'd say that those two events, prove the whole point of having Faith to obey God, gets your ending to always be better than your starting out!

1 Thessalonians 4:13-18 (KJV) But I would not have you to be ignorant, brethren, concerning them which are asleep, that ye sorrow not, even as others which have no hope. 14 For if we believe that Jesus died and rose again, even so them also which sleep in Jesus will God bring with him. 15 For this we say unto you by the word of the Lord, that we which are alive and remain unto the coming of the Lord shall not prevent them which are asleep. 16 For the Lord himself shall descend from heaven with a shout, with the voice of the archangel, and with the trump of God: and the dead in Christ shall rise first: 17 Then we which are alive and remain shall be caught up together with them in the clouds, to meet the Lord in the air: and so shall we ever be with the Lord. 18 Wherefore comfort one another with these words.

In Vs 15, & 17 of the above scripture there is a word there that indicates a lasting power is needed to get caught up. That word is the word "REMAIN." So many people start things, but quit before it's fully finished. When you start school in kindergarten, you never qualify for the diploma because you started. You qualify for the diploma because you remained in school to finish!

If you entered a 200 meters race on Saturday, to qualify for a chance at an Olympic gold medal, but fouled out during the race, because you were tripped by the runner next to you: Although you showed up, was the fastest runner on the field, started the race, but you failed to finish the race. You don't qualify for the olympics! It didn't matter how many pre-qualifying races you had won previously, that weekend. Because you didn't remain in that race, you won't be competing in the Olympics in that category. History will not record your attempts to start, just the facts of how you finished!

Faith to Obey God is not in the starting of anything, but in the full completion of it, in the eyes of God! In the Bible, in the book of 1 Samuel, chapter 15, there is a story that supports this principle; of how you finish in one's obedience to God. King Saul is sent on assignment by the prophet Samuel, to accomplish (finish) a specific assignment for God.

However, in Saul's attempt to finish this specific assignment, Saul listens to the people's request over God's specific commands. Thereby, having Saul fail to finish the assignment on God's terms. Saul figured (human reasoning), that the way God wanted something completed was not the exact way God wanted things done. Have we ever done that after hearing from God? Faith to Obey means to "Obey the GOD way!" If it was asked to be done by God, don't add any human reasoning before it's completed or finished!

1 Samuel 15:1-3 (KJV) Samuel also said unto Saul, The Lord sent me to anoint thee to be king over his people, over Israel: now therefore hearken thou unto the voice of the words of the Lord. 2 Thus saith the Lord of hosts, I remember that which Amalek did to Israel, how he laid wait for him in the way, when he came up from Egypt. 3 Now go and smite Amalek, and utterly destroy all that they have, and spare them not; but slay both man and woman, infant and suckling, ox and sheep, camel and ass.

1 Samuel 15:9-11 (KJV) But Saul and the people spared Agag, and the best of the sheep, and of the oxen, and of the fatlings, and the lambs, and all that was good, and would not utterly destroy them: but every thing that was vile and refuse, that they destroyed utterly. 10 Then came the word of the Lord unto Samuel, saying, 11 It repenteth me that I have set up Saul to be king: for he is turned back from following me, and hath not performed my commandments. And it grieved Samuel; and he cried unto the Lord all night.

1 Samuel 15:18-23 (KJV) And the Lord sent thee on a journey, and said, Go and utterly destroy the sinners the Amalekites, and fight against them until they be consumed. 19 Wherefore then didst thou not obey the voice of the Lord, but didst fly upon

the spoil, and didst evil in the sight of the Lord? 20 And Saul said unto Samuel, Yea, I have obeyed the voice of the Lord, and have gone the way which the Lord sent me, and have brought Agag the king of Amalek, and have utterly destroyed the Amalekites. 21 But the people took of the spoil, sheep and oxen, the chief of the things which should have been utterly destroyed, to sacrifice unto the Lord thy God in Gilgal. 22 And Samuel said, Hath the Lord as great delight in burnt offerings and sacrifices, as in obeying the voice of the Lord? Behold, to obey is better than sacrifice, and to hearken than the fat of rams 23 For rebellion is as the sin of witchcraft, and stubbornness is as iniquity and idolatry. Because thou hast rejected the word of the Lord, he hath also rejected thee from being king.

Am I just a starter of the will of God in My life, but not a finisher on God's terms? There is an interesting discourse between Samuel and Saul, over the obeying of God's commands. The reasoning of man in the completion of obedience to God, can be quite astonishing. Let's first look at what God said about King Saul in verse 10-11, 1 Samuel 15:10-11 (KJV) Then came the word of the Lord unto Samuel, saying, 11 It repenteth me that I have set up Saul to be king: for he is turned back from following me, and hath not performed my commandments. And it grieved Samuel; and he cried unto the Lord all night.

What is so amazing about this discourse, is that I have only found one other time in the word of God, where God is recorded at using the words "it repeneth/repented" in regards to mankind! That was in Genesis 6! Genesis 6:6 (KJV) "And it repented the Lord that he had made man on the earth, and it grieved him at his heart."

Well, we all know what happened after God spoke those words in Genesis... Noah built a boat! Humm... God didn't build a boat with King Saul, but God was done with Saul (and anyone in His family-Generationally) being KING... David is anointed after this. 1 Samuel 15:35 - 16:1 (KJV) And Samuel came no more to see Saul until the day of his death: nevertheless Samuel mourned for Saul: and the Lord repented that he had made Saul king over Israel. 16:1 And the Lord said unto Samuel, How long wilt thou mourn for Saul, seeing I have rejected him from reigning over Israel? fill thine horn with oil, and go, I will send thee to Jesse the Bethlehemite: for I have provided me a king among his sons.

1 Samuel 16:13 (KJV) "Then Samuel took the horn of oil, and anointed him in the midst of his brethren: and the Spirit of the Lord came upon David from that day forward. So Samuel rose up, and went to Ramah." Has God ever thought about saying those same words in the universe of Heaven about me, you, or us today? Does my actions, when it comes to obeying God, fall in the category of rebellion, witchcraft, stubbornness, or idolatry?

1 Samuel 15:23 (KJV)"For rebellion is as the sin of witchcraft, and stubbornness is as iniquity and idolatry. Because thou hast rejected the word of the Lord, he hath also rejected thee from being king." The second thing that stands out is Saul's

answer to Samuel! Saul says something with his mouth, but it is totally reflective of his heart towards God.

1 Samuel 15:14-15 (KJV) And Samuel said, What meaneth then this bleating of the sheep in mine ears, and the lowing of the oxen which I hear? 15 And Saul said, They have brought them from the Amalekites: for the people spared the best of the sheep and of the oxen, to sacrifice unto the Lord thy God; and the rest we have utterly destroyed. Did you see it? It's not the part about the people! Let's read it again, out loud! Just verse 15...

1 Samuel 15:15 (KJV) And Saul said, They have brought them from the Amalekites: for the people spared the best of the sheep and of the oxen, to sacrifice unto the Lord thy God; and the rest we have utterly destroyed. Saul admits that God was NOT his God, only Samuel's God! If God was the God of Saul, then it should have said "unto the Lord OUR, not THY God! I believe that is so key to how we finish! Is it all about God, or us? Am I more concerned about the people's approval, thoughts, or comments, more than my obedience to God?

Think about this, what would it had been like for a finish in the Garden of Eden, if ADAM had said to EVE, when offered the fruit from the tree of the knowledge of Good and Evil..." But God said, Thou shall not eat!?" Talk about its not how you start out, but how you end up! Did you notice, that God never moved in the time period between when EVE had eaten, and when ADAM had not, but only after ADAM had consumed it himself.

With God, there had been a time previously when Adam and God existed without an EVE. So, that meant that GOD needed to see if the helpmate was going to utilize her power of Influence to be a helper, or had the enemy convinced her to become a hinderance, to the God man ADAM (power of Authority) OBEYING the commands of God? Well, we know how the scene plays out (Genesis 3:1-24)

Interestingly, there is never recorded a time when the ADAM male (power of authority), did anything but obey the commands of God, until he had an ADAM female (power of influence) in his presence to be his helper. The enemy made her see the need for herself (self-awareness, not submission to authority), more than the need to obey the commands of God. Both, were "innocent" of Good and Evil before they ate of the fruit, but immediately after eating, their first action was to notice themselves in a naked state, and attempt to cover that physical state of existence (from God, and from themselves i.e. fig leaves). They experienced the spirit of fear (afraid of the presence of God), and exposure in their disobedience. There is a phrase for those actions, its called "Getting what you want, will cost you what you already have!" Notice it doesn't say getting what you NEED!

What is ADAM's answer to God? Genesis 3:10 (KJV) "And he said, I heard thy voice in the garden, and I was afraid, because

I was naked; and I hid myself." I was afraid (fear); I was naked (exposed, revealed); I hid myself (ashamed, seeking to cover up).

Everything ADAM said was all about himself, not God! What is God's response? Genesis 3:11 (KJV) "And he said, Who told thee that thou wast naked? Hast thou eaten of the tree, whereof I commanded thee that thou shouldest not eat?" God's quest is for accountability! Have you noticed, that there is nowhere recorded where ADAM or EVE ever ask for forgiveness, or that they repented! Compare this verse in chapter 3 to Chapter 2! Genesis 2:25 (KJV)"And they were both naked, the man and his wife, and were not ashamed.

So, God is saying to ADAM, "ok you been naked all this time, since you have been here on earth, why is nakedness a big deal today? Did you put your hands in the cookie jar of the tree of the knowledge of Good and Evil, eat one of those cookies (fruit) I told you not to eat?" How different are we today, from becoming finishers with God, or quitters within ourselves, to complete it God's way? Have you ever said, within yourself, "well, surely God didn't really mean it that way, that doesn't make any kind of natural sense? Like Duh! What's natural about God? Isn't God the one that puts the SUPER in the natural?

I think Isaiah 55 says it like this in Isaiah 55:8-9 (KJV) "For my thoughts are not your thoughts, neither are your ways my ways, saith the Lord. 9 For as the heavens are higher than the earth, so are my ways higher than your ways, and my thoughts than your thoughts." This lets me know that Faith to obey God is going to take me some places I could never get to, without God's help, and my ultimate obedience! God already knows what's needed from me, before he asks us to obey, and God already has something (about our task for Him), that will convince others that God is a FINISHER God, not just a starter!

Paul says it this way, Philippians 1:6 (KJV) "Being confident of this very thing, that he which hath begun a good work in you will perform it until the day of Jesus Christ:" Faith to Obey God is about finishing, not just starting!

CHAPTER SIX

We Must Know Our Position As A Believer

Ephesians 6:11-13 (KJV) Put on the whole armour of God, that ye may be able to stand against the wiles of the devil. 12 For we wrestle not against flesh and blood, but against principalities, against powers, against the rulers of the darkness of this world, against spiritual wickedness in high places. 13 Wherefore take unto you the whole armour of God, that ye may be able to withstand in the evil day, and having done all, to stand.

We must know our position as a believer in God, and know that God is not a stranger to the sport of wrestling. Especially tag-team wrestling. However, because of the way that God has set up the system, He cannot legally get involved until we first show up for the match, first in Faith, and second stand up in the ring.

Ephesians 6:13-14 (KJV) "Wherefore take unto you the whole armour of God, that ye may be able to withstand in the evil day, and having done all, to stand.14 Stand therefore, having your loins girt about with truth, and having on the breastplate of righteousness;..."

God doesn't really want us to fight in the earth (flesh/blood) realm (fighting in the spirit realm is where we already have the victory). He just needs us to show up and stand up (in the FAITH ring); as to who we are as a Believer. Then we tag Him (His angels) to do all the Spiritual fighting for us.

Psalms 103:20-21 (KJV) Bless the Lord, ye his angels, that excel in strength, that do his commandments, hearkening unto the voice of his word. 21 Bless ye the Lord, all ye his hosts; ye ministers of his, that do his pleasure. Angels are waiting to hear the word of God to get busy on God's behalf!

In the book of Daniel, we read that Daniel had prayed to God but didn't get his answer until about 3 weeks later. It wasn't that God had not answered, it was that the answer had some spiritual resistance traveling back to Daniel. However, God dispatched

Angels to help out in the fight against the evil spiritual resistance or hangups.

Daniel 10:12-15 (KJV) Then said he unto me, Fear not, Daniel: for from the first day that thou didst set thine heart to understand, and to chasten thyself before thy God, thy words were heard, and I am come for thy words. 13 But the prince of the kingdom of Persia withstood me one and twenty days: but, lo, Michael, one of the chief princes, came to help me; and I remained there with the kings of Persia. 14 Now I am come to make thee understand what shall befall thy people in the latter days: for yet the vision is for many days. 15 And when he had spoken such words unto me, I set my face toward the ground, and I became dumb.

Our position as a believer in God has angelic help! Hebrews 1:14 (KJV)"Are they not all ministering spirits, sent forth to minister for them who shall be heirs of salvation?" The book of Revelation tells us, that only a third of the stars of Heaven were cast to the Earth; so that means that God has two thirds (2/3) still working for him. That also means that "they that be for us, are more than they that be for our enemy!"

Revelation 12:3-4 (KJV) And there appeared another wonder in heaven; and behold a great red dragon, having seven heads and ten horns, and seven crowns upon his heads. 4 And his tail drew the third part of the stars of heaven, and did cast them to the earth: and the dragon stood before the woman which was ready to be delivered, for to devour her child as soon as it was born.

2 Kings 6:15-17 (KJV) And when the servant of the man of God was risen early, and gone forth, behold, an host compassed the city both with horses and chariots. And his servant said unto him, Alas, my master! how shall we do? 16 And he answered, Fear not: for they that be with us are more than they that be with them. 17 And Elisha prayed, and said, Lord, I pray thee, open his eyes, that he may see. And the Lord opened the eyes of the young man; and he saw: and, behold, the mountain was full of horses and chariots of fire round about Elisha.

The book of Revelation also says, one of God's angels trumpets is powerful enough to take out a THIRD of LIFE/ VEGETATION on earth! Think of it this way, if there are six (6) Billion or more people on earth, then a third of six (6) Billion is at least 2 Billion. Let me say it this way, one Angel's trumpet sound = at least 2 BILLION (by the way, how much is two hundred thousand thousand? See Revelation 9:16) gone! 1 Angel = one third (1/3) affected, or 2 BILLION (if 6 billion was the total number). God has two thirds (2/3) of the stars of Heaven on His side, and we have no exact number of how many of them there are; but regardless of how many there are, remember the Bible says ONE (1) angel's trumpet sounds equals 1/3 of trees, part the sea, rivers, sun, moon, stars, night and day Smitten (attacked, or affected). Let me say that again, One of God's angels trumpets sound, and 1/3 of TREES, all GREEN GRASS, Parts of the SEA (Blood, Creatures, Ships), RIVERS, SUN, MOON,

STARS, NIGHT, and DAY affected! Humm, why would anyone not want to know their position as an obedient believer in God? Why would anyone NOT want to be a believer? Like DUH? OMG? REALLY?

Revelation 8 (KJV) And when he had opened the seventh seal, there was silence in heaven about the space of half an hour. 2 And I saw the seven angels which stood before God; and to them were given seven trumpets. 3 And another angel came and stood at the altar, having a golden censer; and there was given unto him much incense that he should offer it with the prayers of all saints upon the golden altar which was before the throne. 4 And the smoke of the incense, which came with the prayers of the saints, ascended up before God out of the angel's hand. 5 And the angel took the censer, and filled it with fire of the altar, and cast it into the earth: and there were voices, and thunderings, and lightnings, and an earthquake. 6 And the seven angels which had the seven trumpets prepared themselves to sound. 7 The first angel sounded, and there followed hail and fire mingled with blood, and they were cast upon the earth: and the third part of trees was burnt up, and all green grass was burnt up. 8 And the second angel sounded, and as it were a great mountain burning with fire was cast into the sea: and the third part of the sea became blood; 9 And the third part of the creatures which were in the sea, and had life, died; and the third part of the ships were destroyed. 10 And the third angel sounded, and there fell a great star from heaven, burning as it were a lamp, and it fell upon the third part of the rivers, and upon the fountains of waters; 11 And the name of the star is called Wormwood: and the third part of the waters became wormwood; and many men died of the waters, because they were made bitter. 12 And the fourth angel sounded, and the third part of the sun was smitten, and the third part of the moon, and the third part of the stars; so as the third part of them was darkened, and the day shone not for a third part of it, and the night likewise. 13 And I beheld, and heard an angel flying through the midst of heaven, saying with a loud voice, Woe, woe, woe, to the inhabiters of the earth by reason of the other voices of the trumpet of the three angels, which are yet to sound!

We will see this same type of affect happening in the victorious leaders of Faith, in this twenty-first century. First, being singled out by their controversial voice, and second, by their uncompromised message to the body of Christ. They will lose "peer" support because of the issues God is calling them to take a stand on. Some of their present conveniences, in this life, will at first seem to be lost, only to be given back to them later, better than they had it before. Victory is defined as the decisive and definitive final triumph over that which challenges you! It's going to be a "good fight of faith," but fear not, for God through Jesus Christ has already given us Victory. Your position is that of Overcomer in your faith to OBEY GOD!

1 Timothy 6:11-12 (KJV) But thou, O man of God, flee these things; and follow after righteousness, godliness, faith, love, patience, meekness. 12 Fight the good fight of faith, lay hold on eternal life, whereunto thou art also called, and hast professed a good profession before many witnesses.

1 John 4:3-6 (KJV) And every spirit that confesseth not that Jesus Christ is come in the flesh is not of God: and this is that spirit of antichrist, whereof ye have heard that it should come; and even now already is it in the world. 4 Ye are of God, little children, and have overcome them: because greater is he that is in you, than he that is in the world. 5 They are of the world: therefore speak they of the world, and the world heareth them. 6 We are of God: he that knoweth God heareth us; he that is not of God heareth not us. Hereby know we the spirit of truth, and the spirit of error.

Paul prays a special prayer, for the position of the believer, in the Book of Ephesians that is worth reading. Ephesians 1:15-23 (KJV) Wherefore I also, after I heard of your faith in the Lord Jesus, and love unto all the saints, 16 Cease not to give thanks for you, making mention of you in my prayers; 17 That the God of our Lord Jesus Christ, the Father of glory, may give unto you the spirit of wisdom and revelation in the knowledge of him: 18 The eyes of your understanding being enlightened; that ye may know what is the hope of his calling, and what the riches of the glory of his inheritance in the saints, 19 And what is the exceeding greatness of his power to us-ward who believe, according to the working of his mighty power, 20 Which he wrought in Christ, when he raised him from the dead, and set him at his own right hand in the heavenly places, 21 Far above all principality, and power, and might, and dominion, and every name that is named, not only in this world, but also in that which is to come: 22 And hath put all things under his feet, and gave him to be the head over all things to the church, 23 Which is his body, the fulness of him that filleth all in all.

This prayer, that Paul prayed, reveals a lot about who we are in God, by Faith. Our position is that of being on top, with everything under our foot. Since Christ is the Head, and we are connected to him, whatever is under His foot is also under our feet. The only things that are not under our feet, are the places we have not placed the soles of our feet on!

Genesis 13:14-17 (KJV) And the Lord said unto Abram, after that Lot was separated from him, Lift up now thine eyes, and look from the place where thou art northward, and southward, and eastward, and westward: 15 For all the land which thou seest, to thee will I give it, and to thy seed for ever. 16 And I will make thy seed as the dust of the earth: so that if a man can number the dust of the earth, then shall thy seed also be numbered. 17 Arise, walk through the land in the length of it and in the breadth of it; for I will give it unto thee.

Abraham had the promise of God that wherever he walked, God would give it to him. How did he walk it? With his feet! Also, we notice that God didn't give him any direction until he was no longer with LOT. Some things, God can't have you do, with Family hanging around you all the time. God desires personal time ALONE with you, not family, times, positioning themselves in your life everywhere you go! If God wanted them with you, HE is well able to tell you to bring them along (without you asking or not obeying until they are with you).

What does Scripture say about Abraham's position with God repeatedly? Exodus 4:2-5 (KJV) And the Lord said unto him, What is that in thine hand? And he said, A rod. 3 And he said, Cast it on the ground. And he cast it on the ground, and it became a serpent; and Moses fled from before it. 4 And the Lord said unto Moses, Put forth thine hand, and take it by the tail. And he put forth his hand, and caught it, and it became a rod in his hand: 5 That they may believe that the Lord God of their fathers, the God of Abraham, the God of Isaac, and the God of Jacob, hath appeared unto thee. (see also Exodus 3:6,15,16)

Not one time does God say he is the God of LOT! Can God say the same thing about your position with HIM? I am the God of _____(insert your name?) Later on, God talks to Joshua as the successor to Moses, and He identifies Moses position with Himself also.

Joshua 1:2-5 (KJV) Moses my servant is dead; now therefore arise, go over this Jordan, thou, and all this people, unto the land which I do give to them, even to the children of Israel. 3 Every place that the sole of your foot shall tread upon, that have I given unto you, as I said unto Moses. 4 From the wilderness and this Lebanon even unto the great river, the river Euphrates, all the land of the Hittites, and unto the great sea toward the going down of the sun, shall be your coast. 5 There shall not any man be able to stand before thee all the days of thy life: as I was with Moses, so I will be with thee: I will not fail thee, nor forsake thee.

Does your Faith to Obey God allow God to say, "As I was with Moses, so I will be with thee _____ (insert your name)!" God was able to say to Joshua, "Wherever you walk is already yours. Why? for two reasons: One, Abraham had already walked it out, and Two, because as Joshua would Obey God, he would not walk anywhere, but where God had already given him the victory!

Is the only reason I haven't stood on my Faith To Obey God, because I don't already know my position as a Believer? If I knew I was Superman, would anyone with a gun shooting at me, stop me from doing my Job? Of course the answer is No! why? Because man's bullets can't hurt Superman! Well, when you know your proper position in the spirit, as a believer, the enemy's misguided strategies (wiles) can't keep you from stepping out in Faith to Obey God either! Use what is already in your hand, and live by what is in your heart towards God! You shield yourself from the enemy's fiery darts with our shield of Faith, not emotions of Fear. Let's look at Eph 1: 20-23 again:

Ephesians 1:20-23 (KJV) Which he wrought in Christ, when he raised him from the dead, and set him at his own right hand in the heavenly places, 21 Far above all principality, and power, and might, and dominion, and every name that is named, not only in this world, but also in that which is to come: 22 And hath put all things under his feet, and gave him to be the head over all things to the church, 23 Which is his body, the fulness of him that filleth all in all.

Jesus Christ is the head, and we (YOU) are his body. The feet are located on the body, When we obey the Head in Faith, wherever he leads us, we must know that we are already empowered in our feet, for the victory! I personally live by the following scriptures below, every day of my life; especially when God trust me to obey HIM in Faith. The "lean not to my own understanding, and be not wise in thine own eyes" parts, are crucial to a believer and one's obedience in order to have proper success in God!

Proverbs 3:5-7 (KJV) Trust in the Lord with all thine heart; and lean not unto thine own understanding. 6 In all thy ways acknowledge him, and he shall direct thy paths. 7 Be not wise in thine own eyes: fear the Lord, and depart from evil.

Encourage all brothers and sisters with this, "Since You ought to Obey God, rather than man; go ahead and put your feet on something, because them feet were made for victory walking. In Jesus name!"

CHAPTER SEVEN

We Must Not Be Concerned About Our Personal Reputation

Have you ever had God, through His Holy Spirit, speak some instructions within you to obey, and your first reaction was, "Oh God, you actually spoke to me?", then it quickly turned to "but OH NOOOO, what will people say if I do that?"

Don't feel bad, God has never been into preserving "our" reputation with Him. Besides, what is it that God doesn't already know about us, anyway? DUH? Seems to me that is what God does on several occasions, when He is ready to test us to obey Him in faith! He tests us on Front street (in front of everyone else to see)!

I often think of Moses and Jonah, when I think of concerns about personal reputations being preserved. Moses was concerned, that he could not do what God was asking Him, because of his speech difficulty. Has that ever been your fear to obey God? You don't like the way you sound verbally, so you believe that God would never want you to be someone that's always in the public eye, or on a platform giving speeches? We read in the book of Exodus, that Moses's speech excuse didn't work well for him, and it even made God angry!

Exodus 4:10-15 (KJV) "And Moses said unto the Lord, O my Lord, I am not eloquent, neither heretofore, nor since thou hast spoken unto thy servant: but I am slow of speech, and of a slow tongue. 11 And the Lord said unto him, Who hath made man's mouth? or who maketh the dumb, or deaf, or the seeing, or the blind? have not I the Lord? 12 Now therefore go, and I will be with thy mouth, and teach thee what thou shalt say. 13 And he said, O my Lord, send, I pray thee, by the hand of him whom thou wilt send. 14 And the anger of the Lord was kindled against Moses, and he said, Is not Aaron the Levite thy brother? I know that he can speak well. And also, behold, he cometh forth to meet thee: and when he seeth thee, he will be glad in his heart."

Since God never changes, according to Malachi 3:6 (KJV) "For I am the Lord, I change not; therefore ye sons of Jacob are not consumed." We can believe that this excuse won't work for us either; today or tomorrow! My mind keeps telling me "Don't even try it!"

Now Jonah was concerned, if he did what God had said, and he operated in his faith to Obey God, he would be known as a false prophet to people; because if what he had told them - didn't come to past, his reputation as a genuine prophet of God was shot! Have you ever been so afraid to obey God, because you were more concerned about what people thought of you, rather than what God already knows about you; before God ever talks to you?

I know I have personally had that same dilemma in my life. Not only just one time! I have had to push, to obey God, regardless of what I will have to endure, because of people. I dealt with that, in writing this very book! Writing this book, is my personal Faith to Obey God test! Just the other day, I was doing a task that God had directed me to do, and while I was doing the task, inside of me I was having a complaining/murmuring session (about how old I was, and who should really being doing this task, and on and on, etc). Then I heard the Holy Spirit interrupt my personal complaining session and ask me two questions. (1). Where does it say come before God with complaining and murmuring? (2). What is it about you giving your opinion, that changes anything in God's word, or God himself? Of course, this is the Holy Spirit being what we would call "Gangster," and "chin checking" a Brother! Ha! What a real in-your-face revelation! No matter what my opinion was about ANYTHING, after I had given it, it hadn't changed a Thing! Or anything in the Bible either! I mean, Psalm 100:4 was the same, after my opinion, as it was before my opinion! Is this what one calls an "Ah Ha" moment?

Psalms 100:4 (KJV)"Enter into his gates with thanksgiving, and into his courts with praise: be thankful unto him, and bless his name." Truth: It reads the same EVERYTIME, regardless of what we (I) say, or think!

Why hadn't I concentrated on the fact, that God had spoken to me that day, to complete a simple task (within my own abilities to do for Him)? Like duh? God trust me that if He asks me to do something for Him, He knew I could do it for Him (I was already capable of OBEYING God). Can God trust you to Obey Him (regardless of people's opinion, or even your own opinion)? That is really powerful! Jesus was trusted that way with God! Remember this verse:

Luke 22:39-44 (KJV) "And he came out, and went, as he was wont, to the mount of Olives; and his disciples also followed him. 40 And when he was at the place, he said unto them, Pray that ye enter not into temptation. 41 And he was withdrawn from them about a stone's cast, and kneeled down, and prayed, 42 Saying, Father, if thou be willing, remove this cup from me: nevertheless not my will, but thine, be done. 43 And there appeared an angel unto him from heaven, strengthening him. 44 And being in an agony he prayed more earnestly: and his sweat was as it were great drops of blood falling down to the ground" Do You think the Angel would have shown up, if God had not heard Jesus' submission of his will? Jesus even taught this obedience lesson to his own disciples:

Matthew 21:28-32 (KJV) "But what think ye? A certain man had two sons; and he came to the first, and said, Son, go work to day in my vineyard. 29 He answered and said, I will not: but afterward he repented, and went. 30 And he came to the second, and said likewise. And he answered and said, I go, sir: and went not. 31 Whether of them twain did the will of his father? They say unto him, The first. Jesus saith unto them, Verily I say unto you, That the publicans and the harlots go into the kingdom of God before you. 32 For John came unto you in the way of righteousness, and ye believed him not: but the publicans and the harlots believed him: and ye, when ye had seen it, repented not afterward, that ye might believe him."

This teaches a great revelation, "your opinion doesn't change a thing, but your obedience to God, will always qualify you for the next assignment from God!" I believe James said something along this same principle in: James 1:22-25 (KJV) "But be ye doers of the word, and not hearers only, deceiving your own selves. 23 For if any be a hearer of the word, and not a doer, he is like unto a man beholding his natural face in a glass: 24 For he beholdeth himself, and goeth his way, and straightway forgetteth what manner of man he was. 25 But whoso looketh into the perfect law of liberty, and continueth therein, he being not a forgetful hearer, but a doer of the work, this man shall be blessed in his deed."

Think about this, The GOD of the entire UNIVERSE that we know, and are discovering, why should HE ever be concerned about our Earthly reputation? It's our spiritual Obedience, that opens the door to eternal blessings! Earthly Reputation before men, or Spiritual Faith To Obey God (FTOG)? We seek so hard to get God's exact word for us to carry out, and when it arrives, we want to pull a Jonah on God! Or even a Moses (I'll get to that one a little later).

Jonah 4:1-3 (KJV) But it displeased Jonah exceedingly, and he was very angry. 2 And he prayed unto the Lord, and said, I pray thee, O Lord, was not this my saying, when I was yet in my country? Therefore I fled before unto Tarshish: for I knew that thou art a gracious God, and merciful, slow to anger, and of great kindness, and repentest thee of the evil. 3 Therefore now, O Lord, take, I beseech thee, my life from me; for it is better for me to die than to live. Really?

Have you ever said this to God? "just take me out of here, I don't want to live anymore? We were more concerned about the outcome in people's eyes, and how we would look to them than in obeying the God of our Universe? Can you believe this about us, if obeying God doesn't turn out in a way that makes us look good (personal reputation) to people, we don't even want to obey GOD!?

Humm... Didn't God just rescue Jonah from the belly of the great fish earlier? Didn't Jonah end up having to do what was asked of him anyway, before he became a fish sandwich? Like DUH? What be the moral of this story then? God is going to get what He wants, from us, regardless of what He has to let us go through to accomplish it! But, there is a "BUT" to this also!

But? Yes BUT! The prophet DANIEL is the but! How so? Let's look at the story of Daniel from King Darius's view. In Daniel chapter 6, we read of the famous Daniel in the lion's den story. But was that story for Daniel, or King Darius? I'd like to say it was for both! Why? Well, I have to go back to Chapter three (3) to set the background. In Chapter three (3), we have the famous story of Hananiah, Mishael (if you turn that "s" into a "c" its the word Michael), and Azariah. These names have been better known as Shadrach, Meshach, and Abednego!

Daniel 1:6-7 (KJV) "Now among these were of the children of Judah, Daniel, Hananiah, Mishael, and Azariah: 7 Unto whom the prince of the eunuchs gave names: for he gave unto Daniel the name of Belteshazzar; and to Hananiah, of Shadrach; and to Mishael, of Meshach; and to Azariah, of Abednego."

Chapter three (3) is known as the Fiery Furnace chapter of the Bible! The famous Babylonian King Nebuchadnezzar's golden image appears. It all seems so fitting from Daniel chapters 2-3, how one event led to another. In Chapter two (2) the King has this dream that he wants interpreted, or he will kill all the Chaldeans, even to cut them into pieces, and their houses made into a dunghill if they don't give the King what he desires. Daniel seeks God for the answers for the king, God delivers, and Daniel saves the day for everyone!

But what did Daniel really do? Daniel told King Nebuchadnezzar that his dream was about him, being the head of Gold, on the great image! Humm, ok, so if I had never told you, that you were the head of Gold, on a great image in Chapter two (2), would you King "Neb" have made the 90 ft tall x 9 ft wide image in Chapter three (3) that you wanted everyone to fall down and worship? So, let me get this right. Daniel tells King Neb about a great image that he is the head of Gold, on top of, in Chapter two (2), and his three friends end up getting thrown into a Fiery furnace in Chapter (3), because you told the king in Chapter (2), he saw an image of himself in a dream! Humm... Connected, or not?

Hey, but there is more, consider this: Daniel is personally responsible for his 3 friends (Shad, Mesh, and Abed) having the great positions they had in Babylon. However, Daniel interprets the dream, but never gets thrown in the Fiery furnace with his Jewish friends.... Humm? Daniel 2:49 (KJV) "Then Daniel requested of the king, and he set Shadrach, Meshach, and Abednego, over the affairs of the province of Babylon: but Daniel sat in the gate of the king."

So, when King Neb, had the music play, and all the people were to fall down and worship, why was only 3 Jews caught not bowing down? Humm? Daniel 3:7-8 (KJV) "Therefore at that time, when all the people heard the sound of the cornet, flute, harp, sackbut, psaltery, and all kinds of musick, all the people, the nations, and the languages, fell down and worshipped the golden image that Nebuchadnezzar the king had set up. 8 Wherefore at that time certain Chaldeans came near, and accused the Jews."

If all the people were to fall down and worship, and there were at least 4 Jews there in leadership (Daniel, Shad, Mesh, and Abed), why did they only point out just 3? Why didn't they include Daniel as one that wasn't falling down... Unless? Humm? I'm just asking?

Daniel 3:9-12 (KJV) "They spake and said to the king Nebuchadnezzar, O king, live for ever. 10 Thou, O king, hast made a decree, that every man that shall hear the sound of the cornet, flute, harp, sackbut, psaltery, and dulcimer, and all kinds of musick, shall fall down and worship the golden image: 11 And whoso falleth not down and worshippeth, that he should be cast into the midst of a burning fiery furnace. 12 There are certain Jews whom thou hast set over the affairs of the province of Babylon, Shadrach, Meshach, and Abednego; these men, O king, have not regarded thee: they serve not thy gods, nor worship the golden image which thou hast set up."

Where was Daniel in all this? Was he not around, not there, off praying in his room everytime the music played, or had he fallen down in the King's presence to not be acused by the Chaldeans? The Bible doesn't tell us, but the Bible does let us know that Daniel had his own separate test of Faith, unlike anyone else in the bible! THERE IS NO ONE ELSE IN THE BIBLE THAT HAS EVERY BEEN KNOWN TO HAVE TO GO TO A LION'S DEN, BUT DANIEL! (Daniel chapter 6).

So when I asked earlier, was the lion's den test for King Darius, or Daniel? I said both! Why would God let the 3 Jewish (Shad, Mesh, and Abed) companions of Daniel, go through such a drastic test of Faith and Loyalty, and have none of the same magnitude for Daniel? I mean wasn't it Daniel who interpreted the original dream in the first place? I mean they all prayed together for the answer, but God used Daniel to speak up.

Daniel 2:17-19 (KJV) "Then Daniel went to his house, and made the thing known to Hananiah, Mishael, and Azariah, his companions: 18 That they would desire mercies of the God of heaven concerning this secret; that Daniel and his fellows should not perish with the rest of the wise men of Babylon. 19 Then was the secret revealed unto Daniel in a night vision. Then Daniel blessed the God of heaven."

The book of Daniel Chapter six (6) starts off with Daniel being under his third (3rd) King, King Darius. Daniel had already served under Nebuchadnezzar, and Belshazzar. Daniel's reputation is on the line now, with others watching every move he made.

Daniel 6:1-5 (KJV) "It pleased Darius to set over the kingdom an hundred and twenty princes, which should be over the whole kingdom; 2 And over these three presidents; of whom Daniel was first: that the princes might give accounts unto them, and the king should have no damage. 3 Then this Daniel was preferred above the presidents and princes, because an excellent spirit was in him; and the king thought to set him over the whole realm. 4 Then the presidents and princes sought to find occasion against Daniel concerning the kingdom; but they could find none occasion nor fault; forasmuch as he was faithful, neither was there any error or fault found in him. 5 Then said these men, We shall not find any occasion against this Daniel, except we find it against him concerning the law of his God."

Wow, what a rep! Wouldn't that be awesome if ALL Christians had that reputation! Boy, wouldn't that be a great testimony for the Kingdom of God, here on Earth. That reputation would really help us all fulfill Matt 6:10! Matthew 6:10 (KJV) "Thy kingdom come. Thy will be done in earth, as it is in heaven." What a God concept! The Creator's Creations doing the things the Creator wanted done, the Creator's way! Anyway, back to Daniel chapter 6. Daniel is set up for a fall by those not of his nationality, because of jealousy, envy, and an outright quest for power!

Daniel 6:6-9 (KJV) "Then these presidents and princes assembled together to the king, and said thus unto him, King Darius, live for ever. 7 All the presidents of the kingdom, the governors, and the princes, the counsellors, and the captains, have consulted together to establish a royal statute, and to make a firm decree, that whosoever shall ask a petition of any God or man for thirty days, save of thee, O king, he shall be cast into the den of lions. 8 Now, O king, establish the decree, and sign the writing, that it be not changed, according to the law of the Medes and Persians, which altereth not. 9 Wherefore king Darius signed the writing and the decree."

Verse 7 is so key, they use the word "ALL" but we know Daniel who was set over all of them, was never included in that all consultation meeting, they were supposed to representing to the King. But, how was the King to know that they were approaching him, having not included Daniel in their counsel before they approached the King? When you have a God reputation, don't be surprised when it get's tested by the enemy; that test will prove how good God is, regardless of us!

Praying to God when times are good, is the foundation for having prayers answered, when times turn difficult. I'm positive that, because Daniel had been a praying man BEFORE the Lion's Den experience, his praying in the Lion's den was not a new adventure! The whole Lion's Den experience for Daniel, got him to Know God in a whole new way, that he had never or would never forget! Think about it this way, being captured to be in Babylon for 70 years, was nothing compared to being in a lion's den overnight! I'm thinking that when Daniel was in that lion's den, he wasn't concerned about which direction Jerusalem was either, like he was in verse 10.

Daniel 6:10 (KJV) "Now when Daniel knew that the writing was signed, he went into his house; and his windows being open in his chamber toward Jerusalem, he kneeled upon his knees three times a day, and prayed, and gave thanks before his God, as he did aforetime." The lesson learned here is, when you go through certain things in Faith with God, relationship becomes more important than religious practice.

God proves to Daniel, that because he had a relationship with God, BEFORE he was facing his most death defying situation of his life, God shows Daniel that HE has a relationship with Daniel, IN his most death defying situation. Daniel saw his God do all night, what man had never seen done all day! Daniel saw an Angel shut the mouths of lions, when there was NO WAY of human escape!

Daniel 6:21-22 (KJV) "Then said Daniel unto the king, O king, live for ever. 22 My God hath sent his angel, and hath shut the lions' mouths, that they have not hurt me: forasmuch as before him innocency was found in me; and also before thee, O king, have I done no hurt."

If the guys that caused Daniel to be cast into the Lion's den, was concerned about Daniel's reputation before the Lion's Den, well, what do you think the talk about town was going to be now, AFTER the lion's den? Hey, aren't we are still talking about Daniel today (some 2555 years later)! Why was Daniel singled out in Chapter six(6),[1] to go thru this monumental trial of Faith in God, like no other? Notice what King Darius says at the end of Daniel's trial in verse 25-28.

Daniel 6:25-28 (KJV) "Then king Darius wrote unto all people, nations, and languages, that dwell in all the earth; Peace be multiplied unto you. 26 I make a decree, That in every dominion of my kingdom men tremble and fear before the God of Daniel: for he is the living God, and stedfast for ever, and his kingdom that which shall not be destroyed, and his dominion shall be even unto the end. 27 He delivereth and rescueth, and he worketh signs and wonders in heaven and in earth, who hath delivered Daniel from the power of the lions. 28 So this Daniel prospered in the reign of Darius, and in the reign of Cyrus the Persian.

What God did with Daniel was more than just for Daniel; it was for King Darius too! King Darius represented the power system of that day, so what he said carried much weight for that day and time zone! All in the Kingdom needed to know that Daniel's God IS GOD! Can God use us to promote himself to the world? There is no man's reputation that can ever stand up to the power of God! When we are able to die to who we think we ought to be, God raises us up to become who we really are!

Now, about Moses! I hadn't forgot. What did I mean about pulling a Moses? Let's look at Numbers 20. This is the famous Second water from the rock story! The first one is contained in Exodus 17:6. This is the second time that Moses has to deal with "People" complaining to him, about what they don't have for themselves! This time, even though Moses is called before God, and given EXACT instructions from God on what to do! Verse 8 is key:

Numbers 20:7-8 (KJV) "And the Lord spake unto Moses, saying, 8 Take the rod, and gather thou the assembly together, thou, and Aaron thy brother, and speak ye unto the rock before their eyes; and it shall give forth his water, and thou shalt bring forth to them water out of the rock: so thou shalt give the congregation and their beasts drink"

Moses didn't even have to ask God for the answer, God gave it to him! "Just speak to the rock (just like I just spoke to you)!" However, Moses doesn't do the update from God. Moses operates in the same thing he had done in the past! He smites the rock, the same way he had operated in God back in Exodus 17:6. Same God, same people, same situation, same Moses, updated instructions, same old obedience, same results! What happened? Immediate judgement!

Numbers 20:11-13 (KJV) "And Moses lifted up his hand, and with his rod he smote the rock twice: and the water came out abundantly, and the congregation drank, and their beasts also. 12 And the Lord spake unto Moses and Aaron, Because ye believed me not, to sanctify me in the eyes of the children of Israel, therefore ye shall not bring this congregation into the land which I have given them."

What happened? Moses leaves the presence of God, with a God given answer for the people of God, and Moses's anger issues, causes him to miss proper obedience to God. It's the ole Spirit verses Flesh battle! Look at verse 10 Numbers 20:10 (KJV) "And Moses and Aaron gathered the congregation together before the rock, and he said unto them, Hear now, ye rebels; must we fetch you water out of this rock?"

Moses leaves the presence of God, and when he gets back around the people, the first thing out of his mouth, is NOT to the rock, but calling God's people names! But, before we get really critical of this great Moses mishap, look at verse 1: Numbers 20:1 (KJV) "Then came the children of Israel, even the whole congregation, into the desert of Zin in the first month: and the people abode in Kadesh; and Miriam died there, and was buried there." Moses had just lost his only sister! The girl that watched over him when he was pulled out of the water, and had been given the name Moses by Pharaoh's Daughter.

Exodus 2:5-10 (KJV) "And the daughter of Pharaoh came down to wash herself at the river; and her maidens walked along by the river's side; and when she saw the ark among the flags, she sent her maid to fetch it. 6 And when she had opened it, she saw the child: and, behold, the babe wept. And she had compassion on him, and said, This is one of the Hebrews' children. 7 Then said his sister to Pharaoh's daughter, Shall I go and call to thee a nurse of the Hebrew women, that she may nurse the child for thee? 8 And Pharaoh's daughter said to her, Go. And the maid went and called the child's mother. 9 And Pharaoh's daughter said unto her, Take this child away, and nurse it for me, and I will give thee thy wages. And the woman took the child, and nursed it. 10 And the child grew, and she brought him unto Pharaoh's daughter, and he became her son. And she called his name Moses: and she said, Because I drew him out of the water."

Faith To Obey God

Moses had just lost family, and all the people wanted was water! It doesn't even say they mourned for Miriam! This is Moses family, and they are complaining to him about what they want! This is not the first time they are complaining to him either. Now, even if they didn't take time to mourn for Miriam, at least let Moses have some time to deal with the lost of his older sister, Right? Wrong, so Moses comes from the presence of God, and he has the word of God in his understanding, but... His feelings get the best of him, and he does not HONOR God in the presence of the people, instead he let's them have a piece of his emotions! Humm, have we ever done that same thing? Prayed all night, or fasted for 3 days to get an answer from God, and then when we get around people, we let them cause us to "pull a Moses"? We let them get us into an emotional state instead of staying covered in God?

Even though Moses, does not honor God properly in his obedience, God still provides for the people, he just holds both Moses and Aaron responsible. So, was it worth it, to let one's emotions rule their actions? I think not! Look at this again, in numbers chapter 20, it opens up with Moses loosing his older sister Miriam, but it closes with Moses loosing his older Brother Aaron too! In one whole chapter in Moses life, he looses his entire family... you think this was an emotional family moment for him?

Lesson Learned: Don't let people get you emotional when you are carrying a word from God!" Don't pull a Moses!

Numbers 20:25-29 (KJV) "Take Aaron and Eleazar his son, and bring them up unto mount Hor: 26 And strip Aaron of his garments, and put them upon Eleazar his son: and Aaron shall be gathered unto his people, and shall die there. 27 And Moses did as the Lord commanded: and they went up into mount Hor in the sight of all the congregation. 28 And Moses stripped Aaron of his garments, and put them upon Eleazar his son; and Aaron died there in the top of the mount: and Moses and Eleazar came down from the mount. 29 And when all the congregation saw that Aaron was dead, they mourned for Aaron thirty days, even all the house of Israel."

The Great Deliverer Moses got to see the promised Land, but never got to go into it! Was it his emotional anger that was his krytonite? (1) He killed a man in Egypt, (2) he smashed the original ten commandments (that God had written), (3) and he hit the rock instead of speaking to it! Humm, seems like his uncontrolled emotions maybe a pattern.

(1) Exodus 2:11-15 (KJV) "And it came to pass in those days, when Moses was grown, that he went out unto his brethren, and looked on their burdens: and he spied an Egyptian smiting an Hebrew, one of his brethren. 12 And he looked this way and that way, and when he saw that there was no man, he slew the Egyptian, and hid him in the sand. 13 And when he went out the second day, behold, two men of the Hebrews strove together: and he said to him that did the wrong, Wherefore smitest thou thy fellow? 14 And he said, Who made thee a prince and a judge

over us? intendest thou to kill me, as thou killedst the Egyptian? And Moses feared, and said, Surely this thing is known. 15 Now when Pharaoh heard this thing, he sought to slay Moses. But Moses fled from the face of Pharaoh, and dwelt in the land of Midian: and he sat down by a well."

(2) Exodus 32:15-19 (KJV) "And Moses turned, and went down from the mount, and the two tables of the testimony were in his hand: the tables were written on both their sides; on the one side and on the other were they written. 16 And the tables were the work of God, and the writing was the writing of God, graven upon the tables. 17 And when Joshua heard the noise of the people as they shouted, he said unto Moses, There is a noise of war in the camp. 18 And he said, It is not the voice of them that shout for mastery, neither is it the voice of them that cry for being overcome: but the noise of them that sing do I hear.19 And it came to pass, as soon as he came nigh unto the camp, that he saw the calf, and the dancing: and Moses' anger waxed hot, and he cast the tables out of his hands, and brake them beneath the mount."

(3) Numbers 20:10-11 (KJV) "And Moses and Aaron gathered the congregation together before the rock, and he said unto them, Hear now, ye rebels; must we fetch you water out of this rock? 11 And Moses lifted up his hand, and with his rod he smote the rock twice: and the water came out abundantly, and the congregation drank, and their beasts also".

Just a note about reputation, if God was concerned about our Earthly reputation over our Spiritual obedience, you think Paul the apostle, who wrote almost a third of Holy Bible, would have qualified?

Last note on earthly reputation vs spiritual obedience: I'm still trying to find in the Bible, where it is that before you can be qualified by God, to be used supernaturally, you must have a man approved theological degree? Let me see, which one of the original (or replacement for Judas) disciples, that Jesus hand picked, had their degree from a theological seminary, before they were effective in their obedience as a follower of Christ? Is it true, that many of those that go to school for ministry, quit the ministry also? So much for earthly reputation! What happens to all the earthly schooling, compared to the Spiritual Obedience? Did we go to school for God (or ourselves), and God told us to quit working in ministry (or did we tell God we were quitting)?

Faith to Obey God means, I must not be concerned about my personal reputation among men (their approval over God's obedience)!

CHAPTER EIGHT

We Must Know To Trust God Beyond Our Natural Understanding(s)

John 4:24 (KJV) "God is a Spirit: and they that worship him must worship him in spirit and in truth." And Romans 8:8 (KJV) "So then they that are in the flesh cannot please God." These scriptures teach us volumes about God and ourselves. First, it teaches us clearly, what we are not able to do with God. We cannot please God in our flesh! Second, the scriptures outline how to properly communicate (worship) with God, IN SPIRIT! However, as simple as this is in theory, it is not that simple in execution, because of a thing we call "having a good understanding of the principle of Why?" I have found that in having Faith To Obey God (FTOG), understanding the "why," mostly always comes after the obedience, never before. Sometimes, the "why" may never come to our human level; but that should never prevent our obedience when it comes to God. Let me repeat something I mentioned earlier. The Bible clearly says that God operates on another level than us, and our limited Human scope of understandings!

Isaiah 55:8-9 (KJV) For my thoughts are not your thoughts, neither are your ways my ways, saith the Lord. 9 For as the heavens are higher than the earth,so are my ways higher than your ways, and my thoughts than your thoughts. Solomon, in the book of Ecclesiastes 12:7 (KJV) says "Then shall the dust return to the earth as it was: and the spirit shall return unto God who gave it." Also in Genesis, God himself, tells the human man named Adam that his flesh is dust!

Genesis 3:19 (KJV)" In the sweat of thy face shalt thou eat bread, till thou return unto the ground; for out of it wast thou taken: for dust thou art, and unto dust shalt thou return." Just for the sake of awareness, the word dust in the Hebrew language is translated as the same word in each of these usages in Genesis and Ecclesiastes!

In the Garden of Eden, in the judgement of the betrayal of God's ultimate command to Adam and Eve, it records something worth considering that could qualify as going beyond our natural understanding. To the Serpent, God points out his new position in its interaction with mankind, or humans. Note: it must have not been a strange occurrence for the serpent to speak, because it doesn't record that Eve was in any way shocked, to listen to the serpent communicating with her. How long had the serpent been previously talking, or was it just that only period that's recorded? Humm? Anyway, God adjust the relationship levels between the serpent and Humans, but he does not change access. He just adjusts the HOW!

In Genesis 3:14 (KJV)" And the Lord God said unto the serpent, Because thou hast done this, thou art cursed above all cattle, and above every beast of the field; upon thy belly shalt thou go, and "dust" shalt thou eat all the days of thy life: Considering that the same Hebrew word for dust, is used in Genesis 3:14 for the serpent to eat, makes an interesting thought of how the enemy was able to be granted the power to inflect boils on the body of Job! Humm? Dust shall thou eat!

Job 2:6-8 (KJV) "And the Lord said unto Satan, Behold, he is in thine hand; but save his life. 7 So went Satan forth from the presence of the Lord, and smote Job with sore boils from the sole of his foot unto his crown. 8 And he took him a potsherd to scrape himself withal; and he sat down among the ashes."

In Strong's version of the King James Bible it reads: Genesis 2:7 (KJV Strong's)"And the Lord God formed man of the dust[h6083.'âpâr][2] of the ground, and breathed into his nostrils the breath of life; and man became a living soul." And Genesis 3:14 (KJV Strong's)"And the Lord God said unto the serpent, Because thou hast done this, thou art cursed above all cattle, and above every beast of the field; upon thy belly shalt thou go, and dust[h6083. 'âpâr] shalt thou eat all the days of thy life:" And Genesis 3:19 (KJV Strong's)"In the sweat of thy face shalt thou eat bread, till thou return unto the ground; for out of it wast thou taken: for dust[h6083. 'âpâr] thou art, and unto dust[h6083. 'âpâr] shalt thou return." And Ecclesiastes 12:7 (KJV Strong's)"Then shall the dust[h6083. 'âpâr] return to the earth as it was: and the spirit shall return unto God who gave it."

According to the strong's concordance of Hebrew words, its using the same word for each occurrence of the word DUST. We have become use to saying Flesh or substituting Flesh for the word Dust in our common communication of English words. Interesting, God decreed to the woman that the serpent's seed had access to inflict its venom [bruise] on the heel of mankind, while mankind's seed had the power to bruise the venomous animal's head. Genesis 3:15 (KJV)"And I will put enmity between thee and the woman, and between thy seed and her seed; it shall bruise thy head, and thou shalt bruise his heel."

Have you noticed, at least for me, we don't have any more verbal conversations with snakes since the Garden of Eden? Well, let me say it this way; I don't have any verbal conversations! I have seen people talk to all kinds of animals in this life, but I can't recall them saying, "You know, I need to talk with someone,

I think I will find me a good snake somewhere, that can understand what I'm going thru right now in my life!" Right!

In Job 2:3-7 (KJV) "And the Lord said unto Satan, Hast thou considered my servant Job, that there is none like him in the earth, a perfect and an upright man, one that feareth God, and escheweth evil? and still he holdeth fast his integrity, although thou movedst me against him, to destroy him without cause. 4 And Satan answered the Lord, and said, Skin for skin, yea, all that a man hath will he give for his life. 5 But put forth thine hand now, and touch his bone and his flesh, and he will curse thee to thy face. 6 And the Lord said unto Satan, Behold, he is in thine hand; but save his life. 7 So went Satan forth from the presence of the Lord, and smote Job with sore boils from the sole of his foot unto his crown."

Did you notice in that conversation between Satan and God, that Satan referred to having access to the flesh of mankind as his level of control, over the outcome of man's relationship with God? Not once is the Spirit mentioned in that conversation. The enemy always believes that he is able to influence our relationship with God, thru access to our flesh! Key: The Flesh cannot pleased God! Since God is NOT Flesh, why would He want us to approach Him in something He is not!? The apostle Paul mentions the effects of this, in one of his letters to the church at Corinth.

1 Corinthians 15:50-53 (KJV) "Now this I say, brethren, that flesh and blood cannot inherit the kingdom of God; neither doth

corruption inherit incorruption. 51 Behold, I shew you a mystery; We shall not all sleep, but we shall all be changed, 52 In a moment, in the twinkling of an eye, at the last trump: for the trumpet shall sound, and the dead shall be raised incorruptible, and we shall be changed. 53 For this corruptible must put on incorruption, and this mortal must put on immortality."

These scriptures references above support the principle that trying to understand God with our flesh, is not how we please or worship God. In Hebrews 11:6 (KJV)"But without faith it is impossible to please him: for he that cometh to God must believe that he is, and that he is a rewarder of them that diligently seek him." This tells us that Faith is the key to pleasing God. We read earlier that to worship God, it must be done in spirit, not the flesh. So, that lets me know to even get into the ballpark with God, it is not done in or with the flesh.

When I think of understanding God, it can't be done with the natural mind! Understanding God is never the criteria for Obeying God. Operating in Faith is! Trusting God is not a human mind issue, but a Heart issue. In the book of Proverbs 3:5-7 (KJV) it says these words"Trust in the Lord with all thine heart; and lean not unto thine own understanding. 6 In all thy ways acknowledge him, and he shall direct thy paths. 7 Be not wise in thine own eyes: fear the Lord, and depart from evil." That is a mouth full of wisdom all by itself!

How often have we trusted the car salesman with our own understanding, and got taken, for the NOT best auto deal possible? WHY do we trust the salesmen over God? I have come to live daily by this word from God in Proverbs 3:5-7, every day of my life! I put it in my cars, and even on my alarm control in my house. I can't go anywhere in my day, without those words facing me as I drive throughout my day! Also, it's the last thing I read before I leave my house, setting the alarm system while I'm gone, and the first thing I read, as I come in the house to clear the alarm code.

I remind myself, that my heart needs to put its trust in God, not the circumstances I maybe facing. I have also learned to "discern in the spirit," what is behind the situation that's facing me with the people, I come into contact with. Regardless, how people are acting, I ask the Holy Spirit of God, to reveal to me who is the "puppet master" pulling the strings of the human puppets, I'm facing at that particular moment. I must be wise enough to know what spiritual battle I'm facing, in the good fight of faith that day.

One of the greatest example of the puppet master, behind the puppet (at least to me), was the scene in the movie, "The Wizard of OZ (1939)," when the dog "Toto" went behind the curtain to reveal the man, on the controls of making the "OZ" look so formidable. Once revealed, their (Dorothy, Tinman, Scarecrow, and the cowardly Lion) positional insights of reaction changed! The bible speaks of God revealing the same thing about Lucifer here:

"Isaiah 14:12-17 (KJV) How art thou fallen from heaven, O Lucifer, son of the morning! how art thou cut down to the ground, which didst weaken the nations!13 For thou hast said in thine heart, I will ascend into heaven, I will exalt my throne above the stars of God: I will sit also upon the mount of the congregation, in the sides of the north:14 I will ascend above the heights of the clouds; I will be like the most High. 15 Yet thou shalt be brought down to hell, to the sides of the pit. 16 They that see thee shall narrowly look upon thee, and consider thee, saying, Is this the man that made the earth to tremble, that did shake kingdoms; 17 That made the world as a wilderness, and destroyed the cities thereof; that opened not the house of his prisoners?

Isn't it always the little things that cause the most irritations? Did you notice above how many times where the focus is on self, using the words "I will"? This clues me into listening to people talking, and how much their conversation is about themselves! Key: Is that a spirit of the enemy operating in a life of self-centeredness, or self-awareness to be combined with self-conceitedness? Is that the same thing the enemy did to Eve in the garden? He changed her awareness away from God's Command, to her own self-awareness! How much did she point out what the forbidden tree would DO for HERSELF before she partook?

Genesis 3:6 (KJV)"And when the woman saw that the tree was good for food, and that it was pleasant to the eyes, and a tree to be desired to make one wise, she took of the fruit thereof, and did eat, and gave also unto her husband with her; and he did eat." Good for food = lust of the Flesh. Have you ever been on a fast, and as soon as you go on your fast, the commercial comes out showing you the most delicious looking sandwich that is NOW available "for a LIMITED time"? Whose Flesh is being tempted with feeding it food? Jesus passed this same test in the wilderness, when he was tempted by saying the words:

Matthew 4:4 (KJV)"But he answered and said, It is written, Man shall not live by bread alone, but by every word that proceedeth out of the mouth of God." (See also Deut 8:3) This always says to me, that I can't live truly for God, if all I am ever concerned about is always feeding my Flesh! I must Obey God's commands, OVER providing for my fleshly needs!

Pleasant to the Eyes = Lust of the eyes. Man, oh man are we ever tempted by something we see with our eyes! Think about this; all the strips clubs and prostitution businesses are built on the capturing of the desires of the eyes! I mean, think about this, have you ever seen an ugly stripper? They don't exist! Everything in the body building industry, is about getting our ole bodies into pleasant looking shape on the outside, more than on the inside. The Plastic surgeon (NIP and TUCK), is all about getting this flesh to become pleasant to the eyes. Think about the money that is invested into our flesh, to have it be pleasant to our own, and/or somebody else's eyes? Have you ever bought a gym membership in Jan of the new year, and you still haven't gone to the gym by April? Well, maybe you just went the first 2 months, but they still charge you rather you show up or not! How much does that good ole daily MIRROR we look at, effect what we call Pleasant to the Eyes? How often are we persuaded to do things by "what we see with our eyes"?

Jesus passed this EYE test also in the wilderness, Matthew 4:8-10 (KJV) "Again, the devil taketh him up into an exceeding high mountain, and sheweth him all the kingdoms of the world, and the glory of them; 9 And saith unto him, All these things will I give thee, if thou wilt fall down and worship me. 10 Then saith Jesus unto him, Get thee hence, Satan: for it is written, Thou shalt worship the Lord thy God, and him only shalt thou serve." (See also Deut 6:13)

Desired to make one wise = Pride of Life. How much do we do things in our life just for us? Have you ever heard of someone saying, I NEED some "ME" time! It's about me, or Them. No one else but themselves, or ourselves! It's all about ME! Have you ever heard someone tell you that YOU better look out for YOURSELF! Ain't NOBODY going to look out for you better in life, than YOU! YOU BETTER TAKE CARE OF YOU! How often do we gravitate to things and people, who tells us how we can make ourselves BETTER for us? Not make ourselves better, just for being better in every area of our lives, but in this one particular area that we feel we need for ourselves!

Jesus passed this test also Matthew 4:5-7 (KJV) "Then the devil taketh him up into the holy city, and setteth him on a pinnacle of the temple, 6 And saith unto him, If thou be the Son of God, cast thyself down: for it is written, He shall give his angels charge concerning thee: and in their hands they shall bear thee up, lest at any time thou dash thy foot against a stone. 7 Jesus said unto him, It is written again, Thou shalt not tempt the Lord thy God."(see also Ps 91:11)

Pride says to God that YOU don't need Him! You know what is better for you than He does, yet He is the one that created you! Pride leads to rebellion, and rebellion ends up in Rejection! We all know that God hates Pride. The right way to approach God is through submission and humility. Proverbs 6:16-19 (KJV) "These six things doth the Lord hate: yea, seven are an abomination unto him:17 A proud look, a lying tongue, and hands that shed innocent blood, 18 An heart that deviseth wicked imaginations, feet that be swift in running to mischief, 19 A false witness that speaketh lies, and he that soweth discord among brethren." And James 4:7-8 (KJV) "Submit yourselves therefore to God. Resist the devil, and he will flee from you. 8 Draw nigh to God, and he will draw nigh to you. Cleanse your hands, ye sinners; and purify your hearts, ye double minded."

Key: there is no resisting of the Devil, if you are not first submitted to God! Adam and Eve proved this in the Garden of Eden, and Jesus provided the better choices in His wilderness journey. Same enemy giving the same test (more than once), but the difference was Jesus was submitted to God by the Holy

Spirit, and not to his flesh. Adam and Eve submitted to the flesh, and not the Spirit of God in obedience!

Note: In the wilderness test of Jesus it is recorded in both Matt 4, and Luke 4. However, the sequence of the testing is different, but it proves that the enemy has no NEW test for us, but the same ole ones that first worked in the Garden in Genesis. They were Lust of the Flesh (LOF), Pride of Life (POL), and Lust of Eyes (LOE). In Matt 4 the order is LOF, POL, LOE. However, in Luke 4 the order is LOF, LOE, POL. Its interesting to note that in the Genesis account it is LOF, LOE, and POL also! What is even more distinguished is that the LOF is always the first temptation? Humm, does that mean that the enemy knows we are always concerned more about pleasing our flesh over the spirit, and that the FLESH CAN NOT PLEASE GOD! WOW!

John said it this way in his book of 1 John: 1 John 2:15 (KJV) "Love not the world, neither the things that are in the world. If any man love the world, the love of the Father is not in him." Is this what happened in the Garden, and NOT in the wilderness?" 1 John 2:16 (KJV)"For all that is in the world, the lust of the flesh(LOF), and the lust of the eyes(LOE), and the pride of life(POL), is not of the Father, but is of the world."

I want to close this chapter with some bible examples of three people, who had FTOG beyond their understanding. These names maybe familiar to you, but is their testimony of FTOG just as clear? The first one is ISAIAH, most popularly known as a prophet who wrote one of the biggest books in the bible. The book of Isaiah has as many chapters as there are books in the bible. Isaiah has 66 chapters! The Bible has 66 books! He was also known as the son of Amoz, an esteemed citizen of Jerusalem, and is somewhat famous for his conversation with King Hezekiah on the terms limited of how long that king would live. King Uzziah is famously known as the opening of Isaiah's ministry. Isaiah is reported as having been sawn asunder also. There are also some of the most repeated verses, from the book of Isaiah, used in the Church world. This one is just a sample:

Isaiah 1:18-20 (KJV) "Come now, and let us reason together, saith the Lord: though your sins be as scarlet, they shall be as white as snow; though they be red like crimson, they shall be as wool. 19 If ye be willing and obedient, ye shall eat the good of the land: 20 But if ye refuse and rebel, ye shall be devoured with the sword: for the mouth of the Lord hath spoken it." And Isaiah 6:1 (KJV) "In the year that king Uzziah died I saw also the Lord sitting upon a throne, high and lifted up, and his train filled the temple."

Isaiah 38:1-8 (KJV) "In those days was Hezekiah sick unto death. And Isaiah the prophet the son of Amoz came unto him, and said unto him, Thus saith the Lord, Set thine house in order: for thou shalt die, and not live. 2 Then Hezekiah turned his face toward the wall, and prayed unto the Lord, 3 And said, Remember now, O Lord, I beseech thee, how I have walked before thee in truth and with a perfect heart, and have done that which is good in thy sight. And Hezekiah wept sore. 4 Then came the word of the Lord to Isaiah, saying, 5 Go, and say to Hezekiah, Thus saith the Lord, the God of David thy father, I have heard thy prayer, I have seen thy tears: behold, I will add unto thy days fifteen years. 6 And I will deliver thee and this city out of the hand of the king of Assyria: and I will defend this city. 7 And this shall be a sign unto thee from the Lord, that the Lord will do this thing that he hath spoken; 8 Behold, I will bring again the shadow of the degrees, which is gone down in the sun dial of Ahaz, ten degrees backward. So the sun returned ten degrees, by which degrees it was gone down.

There are many more, because there are 66 chapters in this Book! However, I desired to concentrate on one chapter in particular that illustrates the focus of this chapter in FTOG; having one's natural understanding challenged. Have you ever read Isaiah chapter 20? Isaiah 20:2-3 (KJV) "At the same time spake the Lord by Isaiah the son of Amoz, saying, Go and loose the sackcloth from off thy loins, and put off thy shoe from thy foot. And he did so, walking naked and barefoot. 3 And the Lord said, Like as my servant Isaiah hath walked naked and barefoot three years for a sign and wonder upon Egypt and upon Ethiopia;"

Wait, a minute! Just one minute! Did I just read that GOD told the mighty prophet ISAIAH, who wrote 66 chapters in the HOLY Bible, to walk around NAKED for not one, but three years (1,095 days)? Nah, let me read that again! No way, would God ask anything like that of HIS servants! Naked for three years?

Wait a minute, could FTOG mean that God is not concerned about my flesh needs like I am?

For some that may be having a little problem adjusting to that, some theologians have said that Isaiah wasn't completely naked, but was undressed to the point of without outer garments (prophet garments) and just worn a loin cloth around his private parts (the same as when David danced), which was considered as being naked. This was considered a "state of nakedness." This is supported also by reading the same verse of scripture in "several versions" of the bible. One in particular is the Dake's Annotated Reference Bible.[3]

The point is, God told Isaiah to Obey him in a fashion that was not the norm for dressing in that societal age or day. Boy, can you here the religious talking up a storm? No way, would God ask his servants to dress like that! I mean, to this day, don't come to church not dressed in a suit and tie! Everybody wears a tie, doctors, lawyers, school teachers, etc, so why does wearing a tie to church make one any different from those that wear them all week long? Is that religious, or just a good ole Fashion show? Doesn't the bible say that God looks on the inside (the heart)?

1 Samuel 16:7 (KJV) "But the Lord said unto Samuel, Look not on his countenance, or on the height of his stature; because I have refused him: for the Lord seeth not as man seeth; for man looketh on the outward appearance, but the Lord looketh on

the heart." The second subject of discussion, on natural understanding is the prophet Hosea! Put your seat belt on!

Hosea 1:2-3 (KJV) "The beginning of the word of the Lord by Hosea. And the Lord said to Hosea, Go, take unto thee a wife of whoredoms and children of whoredoms: for the land hath committed great whoredom, departing from the Lord. 3 So he went and took Gomer the daughter of Diblaim; which conceived, and bare him a son."

Wait, hold the presses.... Did God just tell his prophet to go marry a prostitute! No way, no religious way did God tell his servant to go find a prostitute, marry her, knowing she loves promiscuous sexual activity! God is never religious, but always relational! Get this: Hosea obeyed God! Hosea exercised his free will by choosing Gomer, of all the choices he may have encountered to choose from, Hosea said to himself, Gomer is the one for me! God never told him to choose Gomer (God said choose one of that occupation), so Gomer must have been pleasant to Hosea's eyes! God was not going to have Hosea, tell him what Adam told Him earlier in the Garden... The woman you gave me! Ha!

Genesis 3:12 (KJV) "And the man said, The woman whom thou gavest to be with me, she gave me of the tree, and I did eat." Gomer was all Hosea's choice, not God's! FTOG does not take away your free will, it just ask us to bend our will, to the desires of God's obedience. Fasting where you eat only fruit, is not the same as eating only strawberries. We still get to choose in how we obey, even in what we obey! Fruit only maybe God's command, what type of fruit is our choice! "Take unto thee a wife of whoredom, that was God. He went and took Gomer, that was on Hosea!

Boy, two powerful examples of God asking his believers/servants to Obey him, in things that were not full of human understanding for that time/day/age. BUT, THEY OBEYED GOD-REGARDLESS!

This last example is probably the most famous of all, to this day! I mean this one is so up there, on the list, that I don't know if it could even be duplicated in the minds of human understanding, even in 2017! I know we are in the age of enlightenment and all that, but still how many men do you know of today that can believe that the girl he is engaged to is pregnant with a baby, but she has not been with a man, and she is claiming that she is still a virgin? Yeah, I'm talking about the story of MARY, the flesh womb mother of Jesus Christ!

I can hear the good ole brothers saying to the sisters nowadays, "Your name is not Mary! Jesus already came, and has gone back! So, who you been with? On top of that, my name is not that guy named Joseph, and I certainly haven't had any angelic dreams, or visions about that baby you are carrying!" Yeah, it took faith then, to obey God in Mary's day, and it would take some Faith today, to do the same thing (even with the new medical advancements procedures from sperm clinics). I mean, if you're engaged to someone to be married, why are you going to a clinic to get someone else's sperm, like duh? And you want him to accept that, you are in love with him only? Right!

However, God didn't care about Mary's reputation, her understanding, or even the threat of her possibly being stoned to death (talk about a big lie going around in that day, can't you hear them now talking at the well, drawing water, Girl, have yah heard about Mary?)! God needed her faith to obey, to affect the destiny of us! When God asks us to have faith in our obedience to Him, he is using us to affect the outcome of many more than just ourselves!

Luke 1:26-35 (KJV) "And in the sixth month the angel Gabriel was sent from God unto a city of Galilee, named Nazareth, 27 To a virgin espoused to a man whose name was Joseph, of the house of David; and the virgin's name was Mary. 28 And the angel came in unto her, and said, Hail, thou that art highly favoured, the Lord is with thee: blessed art thou among women. 29 And when she saw him, she was troubled at his saying, and cast in her mind what manner of salutation this should be. 30 And the angel said unto her, Fear not, Mary: for thou hast found favour with God. 31 And, behold, thou shalt conceive in thy womb, and bring forth a son, and shalt call his name Jesus. 32 He shall be great, and shall be called the Son of the Highest: and the Lord God shall give unto him the throne of his father David: 33 And he shall reign over the house of Jacob for ever; and of his kingdom there shall be no end. 34 Then said Mary unto the angel, How shall this be, seeing I know not a man? 35 And the angel answered and said unto her, The Holy Ghost shall come upon thee, and the power of the Highest shall overshadow thee: therefore also that holy thing which shall be born of thee shall be called the Son of God.

Luke 1:37-38 (KJV) "For with God nothing shall be impossible. 38 And Mary said, Behold the handmaid of the Lord; be it unto me according to thy word. And the angel departed from her."

Matthew 1:18-21 (KJV) "Now the birth of Jesus Christ was on this wise: When as his mother Mary was espoused to Joseph, before they came together, she was found with child of the Holy Ghost. 19 Then Joseph her husband, being a just man, and not willing to make her a public example, was minded to put her away privily. 20 But while he thought on these things, behold, the angel of the Lord appeared unto him in a dream, saying, Joseph, thou son of David, fear not to take unto thee Mary thy wife: for that which is conceived in her is of the Holy Ghost. 21 And she shall bring forth a son, and thou shalt call his name Jesus: for he shall save his people from their sins.

Mary and Joseph illustrate for us, the most common challenge we have in operating in our FTOG. The first response to God (Supernatural) is our natural understanding! "How shall this be, seeing I know not a Man!" On Joseph's part, it says that before he had that angelic dream, he was set on putting her away, just not publically. The man was SET, ha! His natural understanding was working overtime in that situation. Thank

God for Joseph's angelic dream! That's where the earlier reference to Isaiah is needed again.

Isaiah 55:8-9 (KJV) For my thoughts are not your thoughts, neither are your ways my ways, saith the Lord. 9 For as the heavens are higher than the so earth are my ways higher than your ways, and my thoughts than your thoughts. Also the Proverbs' wisdom scripture: Proverbs 3:5-7 (KJV) "Trust in the Lord with all thine heart; and lean not unto thine own understanding. 6 In all thy ways acknowledge him, and he shall direct thy paths. 7 Be not wise in thine own eyes: fear the Lord, and depart from evil."

Well, in FTOG, WE MUST KNOW TO TRUST GOD BEYOND OUR NATURAL UNDERSTANDING(S). In this chapter, I hope you have gained clearer insights on what that could mean in your journey to serve God at a new level. If nothing else, you can be happy that God has not asked you to walk around naked for three (3) years, marry a prostitute, or claim you are pregnant with God's baby!

Can you agree with me, there is not any human understanding even today that helps one believe that this is the will of God for your life! I mean, if you had not just read them for yourself, and every time you go back to the bible they will still be there! Oh wow, I have just one more that maybe will whet your appetite. Let's look at

2 Samuel 12:7-8 (KJV) "And Nathan said to David, Thou art the man. Thus saith the Lord God of Israel, I anointed thee king over Israel, and I delivered thee out of the hand of Saul; 8 And I gave thee thy master's house, and thy master's wives into thy bosom, and gave thee the house of Israel and of Judah; and if that had been too little, I would moreover have given unto thee such-and-such things."

Here in Nathan's exposure of David's sin before God, God has Nathan tell David this, "You didn't have to take things of your flesh into your own hands, I had previously given you all that you had. However, if what I had given you wasn't enough, all you had to do was just ask me for more, I would have given you more!" The lesson learned here is how often do we take things into our own hands because we won't wait on God's way of doing it, or we never asked God first if it was for us?

I get excited over God saying to David, "If I hadn't already given you enough, all you had to do was just ask me for more!" Wow! When your heart is toward God (not your natural understanding), and his way of doing things, God will add unto you as a reward; you don't have to do all this stuff for yourself! Matthew 6:33 (KJV) "But seek ye first the kingdom of God, and his righteousness; and all these things shall be added unto you." And Hebrews 11:6 (KJV) "But without faith it is impossible to please him: for he that cometh to God must believe that he is, and that he is a rewarder of them that diligently seek him."

CHAPTER NINE

Conclusion

My personal goal in writing this book was, to fulfill the personal call God put on my life when I was only 8 years old, and reinforced by Him in my life later, at the age of 25. God told me to "Teach People to Develop a Personal Relationship with God!" So, my hope is that after reading the chapters in this book, you have come into a better relationship with the God of the Bible, not just His Bible! The Bible from Genesis to Revelation is about the Creator and His different levels of RELATIONSHIP (both Good and Bad) with his Creations (both Fully Spiritual and Not-Fully Spiritual).

God's Bible is also a book that describes the many levels at which God is committed to the process of restoration with His creations. In the old testament, Psalm 78 is classic in the summation of the levels by which God has gone thru, in dealing with his "Flesh also" creations, in this restoration process. The Bible is also classic in outlining God's ultimate, full restoration process; called "Jesus Christ!" with His "Flesh also" creation. Jesus was sent to connect us eternally with God, not replace God!

In the new testament, Paul says it this way, about the restoration process, 2 Corinthians 5:18-21 (KJV) "And all things are of God, who hath reconciled us to himself by Jesus Christ, and hath given to us the ministry of reconciliation; 19 To wit, that God was in Christ, reconciling the world unto himself, not imputing their trespasses unto them; and hath committed unto us the word of reconciliation. 20 Now then we are ambassadors for Christ, as though God did beseech you by us: we pray you in Christ's stead, be ye reconciled to God. 21 For he hath made him to be sin for us, who knew no sin; that we might be made the righteousness of God in him."

Timothy says this in 2 Timothy 3:16-17 (KJV) All scripture is given by inspiration of God, and is profitable for doctrine, for reproof, for correction, for instruction in righteousness: 17 That the man of God may be perfect, thoroughly furnished unto all good works. The point here is, that men from God must be inspired by God, in order to become complete in their personal Lives! So, as we come to the end of this writing, on Faith To Obey God (FTOG) what have we learned? Four main things. FTOG is all about Trust, Timing, being Personal, and it can be Controversial!

Do I Trust God above myself? Can God Trust me (as His creation), to obey Him as the creator? In obeying God, I must not only know the What, I need to know the How, and the When also! Timing is so critical with God, that even Jesus says he does not know the when to everything. Jesus said, these very words in Matthew 24:36 (KJV) "But of that day and hour knoweth no man, no, not the angels of heaven, but my Father only."

I must realize that what God is asking me to obey, it is not for anyone else, but me personally. Doing somebody's else job gives me no credit! God is awesome enough, to not need to have duplication of the exact same thing! What God has done, is so magnificent by itself, and He is so good at what he does, He doesn't need to make copies, or do it over. There is a distinct difference between Duplication and Multiplication. Duplication is understood as the same exact thing over and over, whereas Multiplication is known as more of something, not necessarily the same exact thing! When God has something NEW, its new, never having been made "exactly" like that before! God told Adam and Eve to multiply, not duplicate! There maybe more than 6 Billion humans on this planet, but each is unique in its own way, not duplicated as the exact same (like robots).

Genesis 1:27-28 (KJV) "So God created man in his own image, in the image of God created he him; male and female created he them. 28 And God blessed them, and God said unto them, Be fruitful, and multiply, and replenish the earth, and subdue it:

and have dominion over the fish of the sea, and over the fowl of the air, and over every living thing that moveth upon the earth."

THINK ABOUT THIS: What Jesus did at Calvary was so good with God, that there will never be another Jesus having to do it over. Jesus said, "it's finished." It was, has been, and forever is; for all eternity too! Get this, The Devil is so good at what he does in deception, and evil, that there is no need for two Devils! Hallelujah! The Devil is so bad at being bad, that after 1000 years of being locked away, he comes out just as bad as he was, when he went into lock-up 1000 years earlier! Wow!

Revelation 20:1-3 (KJV) "And I saw an angel come down from heaven, having the key of the bottomless pit and a great chain in his hand. 2 And he laid hold on the dragon, that old serpent, which is the Devil, and Satan, and bound him a thousand years, 3 And cast him into the bottomless pit, and shut him up, and set a seal upon him, that he should deceive the nations no more, till the thousand years should be fulfilled: and after that he must be loosed a little season"

Revelation 20:7-10 (KJV) "And when the thousand years are expired, Satan shall be loosed out of his prison, 8 And shall go out to deceive the nations which are in the four quarters of the earth, Gog and Magog, to gather them together to battle: the number of whom is as the sand of the sea. 9 And they went up on the breadth of the earth, and compassed the camp of the saints about, and the beloved city: and fire came down from God out of heaven, and devoured them. 10 And the devil that deceived them was cast into the lake of fire and brimstone, where the beast and the false prophet are, and shall be tormented day and night for ever and ever."

Notice it doesn't say that the fire and brimstone "consumed" them, but tormented them day and night for ever and ever. Humm, a Lake of Fire that burns for all eternity! Wow! If you were consumed, how could you still be tormented? There would be nothing left there to torment, with consumption. A Lake of Fire that never goes out (you think this would add a new dimension to the old 1974 Ohio Players song- FIRE?).

If the stars in the universe are different, each having its own name, and twins don't have the same fingerprint, God is not only awesome, but very personal too! Psalms 147:4-5 (KJV) "He telleth the number of the stars; he calleth them all by their names. 5 Great is our Lord, and of great power: his understanding is infinite."

I can not live My life in the approval of mankind, only God! If I am image-conscious, I'm going to have problems obeying God. If I want to be used by the Supernatural, I can't ask the natural for approval. Supernatural is always controversial with the natural! So, the bottom line is, FTOG is about developing my own personal relationship with the God of the universe, not like anyone one else in creation!

Table 1/ Annex A

SO WHAT ARE SOME TAKE AWAYS FROM ALL OF THIS? HERE IS MY TOP TEN LIST:

1.   FTOG is never about understanding before obeying. I obey first, to get the understanding second.

2.   FTOG is never only about ME, but God using me, to bring a bigger picture of Himself to everyone else.

3.   FTOG has nothing to do with man's approval. Only God's instructions, to be followed, regardless of man's opinion.

4.   FTOG is not about getting a second opinion from man, before I obey God.

5.   FTOG will never be about increasing my popularity with man, but it may bring me into some controversy with mankind.

6.   FTOG will involve more than just me, to be fully accomplished.

7.   FTOG will take God to be involved, in order for the full effect of my obedience, to be realized.

8.   FTOG will not make natural sense, but it will take Faith in God to complete.

9.   FTOG is not defined by what others have done, but only by what God is asking me to accomplish in my own obedience.

10.   FTOG is about fully trusting the Creator, who has created me.

Table 2/ Annex B

103 Things (Insights) I've learned in my Personal Faith to Obey God journey:

AKA: "WISDOM NUGGETS"

1. It has always been about, and it will always be about God- NOT ME! Gen. 1:1

2. God is never surprised at me, as much as I am surprised at myself! Eccl. 1:9

3. I'm so glad - God never changes! Mal. 3:6b

4. God knew me before I knew myself, therefore he uses me based on what he already knew about me when he made me. Ps. 139:13-18

5. Even when I get lost within life, I'm not a lost cause to God! Rom. 5:8, Jeremiah 29:11

6. I'm so glad He is God, and I'm not! Isa. 45:5

7. I love God more for his Powers of Love, Forgiveness, Grace, and Mercy, than any of his other powers. Exod. 34:6-7

8. It is GOD that has made me, and not me myself! Ps. 100:3

9. The more I learn about myself, the more I fall in love with God. Ps. 139 & Ps. 8

10. To be in God's service for anything is the greatest privilege in life!

11. To serve God is the highest position in life.

12. To obey God is the highest reward in life. Deut. 28:1-14

13. To have God speak to me is the highest honor in life.

14. To be saved by the grace of God, is the highest Favor in life! John 3:16, Eph. 2:8

15. My name written in the Lamb's book of life, is the Highest achievement in life! Rev. 13:8

16. The ability to receive the forgiveness of God, and to forgive oneself, is the key to living a fulfilled and successful life. Mark 11:25-26

17. The love of God is not spelled with 4 letters, but 2 words: Grace & Mercy! Lam. 3:22-23

18. God never calls perfect people to work with Him, because he didn't make any! Rom. 3:23 & Ps 51:5.

19. Since God is perfect, he doesn't need me to be perfect; just submitted. 1 Sam. 22:15 & Jeremiah1:4-5

20. No one else's opinions really matters when I am obeying God! Eccl. 12:13-14

21. I am what I am, yet by the Grace of God. 1 Cor. 15:10

22. God's way is the only way that really matters! Prov. 16:2, 19:21

23. When it comes down to my happiness, or getting my way, my arms are too short to box with God.

24. What I fill myself with every day, will come out in my words when I talk. Matt. 12:34-37

25. To stay humble, I must operate in the fruit of the Spirit daily. Gal. 5:23 & Prov. 15:33

26. Pride and Offense are glued together like two sides of the same coin. Matt. 16:23

27. If God didn't deliver Jesus from his cross, don't look to get delivered from my cross.

28. To truly be in the service of God, I have to want to please God more than His people.

29. If I can do what I think God wants me to do without God, then I am not working for God, but myself!

30. The prayer of Repentance is the greatest prayer of healing and restoration that one can pray. 2 Chron. 7:14

31. God never wanted me to know about Him, God wanted me to know him! Job 42:5

32. Who I listen to everyday, ends up being who I serve every day. Gen.3:1-5,17

33. One will never be greater than the spirit that controls them. Gal. 5:19-26

34. Obeying God in my spirit often looks stupid in my flesh Gen. 22:17-18

35. When I am obeying God's will for my life, don't expect to be supported, but criticized. Neh. chapter 4

36. Being Powerful in God will make me unpopular with People (especially family). Jeremiah 4:4-10, 17-19, John 10:31-39. John 15:18-21.

37. What God is silent on, I should be too! Mark 14:60-61.

38. I think too small to only listen to my own thoughts. I need to listen to God's inspirations more than my own thoughts - always. Rom.10:17

39. I'm to valuable to God, to listen to and believe what others say about me. Rom. 10:17

40. What bothers God should bother me, what does not bother God, shouldn't bother me. Numbers 12

41. Keep my focus on God, not on the people! Numbers 14

42. God never delivers by the size in numbers, but by faith and obedience. Judges 7

43. What I see in faith, God can bring to fact. Mark 11:24, Rom. 4:17-22

44. I never build UNITY by exposing differences for the bad, but by appreciating what everyone brings to the table for the good.

45. The sheep belong to God, not me. God owns the range, Jesus is the chief Ranch Handler, the Holy Spirit is the Spiritual watch dog, and I am just a manager (hand) to help!

46. God doesn't need me, I need HIM!

47. Free will is what separates the humans from the animals; yet mankind has not yet proven to be the smartest animal on the planet.

48. What one births will forever have some degree of control over the one that birth's it.

49. It's not always how I start out, or sometimes end up; but really the journey of discovery in between the two (the beginning and the end). Eccl. 7:8

50. The more I know/understand about God, the better I will be able to appreciate oneself.

51. Happiness in God, when I am in the worst of times of my life, means I will be ecstatic in God, in the best of times of my life.

52. People in love have weddings, but the good marriages work because of trust. However, where the trust goes, so goes the relationship!

53. I didn't really know the depth of who God is, until I made mistakes. There are some qualities about God, that only human mistakes can help one understand.

54." Don't be a Soul Saved, and a Life wasted!" Paula White

55. Faith Works by Love Gal 5:6/Mark 11:22

56. "Whatever you make happen for others, God will make happen for you." M. Murdock. Eph. 6:8.

57. The size of my Problem/Challenge, is never as important as the size of Me with my Faith in God. Always compare whatever I'm going through, to the size and Promises of God!-Genesis 18:14b"Is anything too hard for the Lord?"

58. Prepare my vessel for use, more than preparing my message for speaking.

59. God will never compete with me for the operation, control, or direction I want to use in my free will! Gen. 3:8-17. However, God will hold me personally accountable to Him, on how I chose to use my free will
.

60. Doing/fulfilling God's will in my life is not about me, but about God. Always be aware, to not let me get in God's way on how he will use me; to fulfill his will in my life. I'm positive Daniel never prayed for God to send him into a lions den! But both God and Daniel are more famous after the den of lions, than they ever was before it. Dan. 6:25-28

61. Preaching gets me out of the world, but teaching gets the world out of the ME.

62. The ability to survive, has everything to do with my ability to adjust/readjust. Don't get stuck on what worked in the past, be open to new revelation from God, not approved by Man.

63. "Something You Are Believing Is Deciding What You Are Receiving" M.Murdock

64. Many people have an agenda of controlling the events in their life, to their advantage (Right or Wrong).

65. Sin makes you stupid! (How many times do I have to ask myself, "What was I thinking?").

66. The anointing of God is always more powerful than my flesh's weaknesses.

67. God is Sovereign, I am not, so It's All about Him, not me! Matt 6:10

68. Stay focused on who I am following (God), not who is following me (people).

69. Build God's Kingdom, not my personal church!

70. Prioritize my Life, and EVERYTHING I do (DOING), in order to hear these words from God "Well Done, thou good and Faithful Servant."

71. Never allow the influence or pressure of the people I am serving, to get me to disobey direct instructions from God (it didn't work out good for King Saul or Moses). 1 Sam. 15:10-11; Numbers 20:12

72. Pray for the presence of God, more than the presence of people (don't let the people cut my hair - Samson). Judges 16:17-20

73. Everything is seasonal (changes). Learn to recognize which season I am in!

74. Nothing is permanent-Bad times and/or Good times.

75. Key to this Life: Outlast the Season... Don't let the season take me out!

76. God will not trust me with more than I can manage (especially with my mouth).

77. When I am going through... Do I praise or complain? How I talk in a season, is tied to how long that season has to last in my life.

78. God is trying to change ME in the circumstance, before He changes the circumstance.

79. Don't mismanage my private time with God, for a priority with people.

80. Don't live in offense too long. It's not if I will have offense, it's just a matter of when!

81. Forgiveness is not a feeling, it is the KEY action to total freedom.

82. When I can do it all without God's help, its not from God!

83. Take no stowaways with me, they are not for me, they are for themselves.

84. I am are always loved by God-Regardless; so make sure He is #1 in my life!

85. "No one can ever say anything to God about me, that God doesn't already know!" B. Carn

86. Don't just have faith for situations, let Faith have ME!

87. Don't be afraid of making a mistake, be afraid of operating in a spirit of non-repentance.

88. Restoration is for relationships, not religion!

89. People want what they want regardless, so make sure I hear from GOD, before I react with people!

90. People want a WORD from God, but God wants ME to Listen to His VOICE!

91. God's Word is what he has said, God's Voice is what He is Saying-right now.

92. God made me this way for HIS purpose... Not mine.

93. God never created mistake-proof people.

94. The only true way to serve God, is with dead flesh and a delivered spirit! Mark 10:21

95. Leave people, in order to please God, never leave God to please the people. Job 2:9-10, Mark 3:31-35, & Luke 18:24-30

96. When God gives me a God assignment, I can't complete it WITHOUT GOD!

97. God's assignments are from out of this world Phil. 1:6

98. The spirit that controls me, will represent me in my actions and with my mouth.

99. I must listen daily to what God says about who he is to me, and who I am to Him.

100. People never promised to "not" leave me, God did! Heb. 13:5

101. How I utilize my freewill never changes God. Matt 26:39, Gen. 16:2-5

102. Focusing on God, will Move Me from mediocre to Master! Go with God, not people!

103. My next Harvest is tied to the words that come out of my mouth daily! Prov. 18:21

ABOUT THE AUTHOR

Kevin B. Brewer is a retired Military Officer of the United States Marine Corps. He served in both the reserve and active duty forces from December of 1973 to August of 1997. He wore the commissioned officer ranks of Second Lieutenant to Lieutenant Colonel.

While stationed in Okinawa, Japan in 1979, he accepted the call of God on his life, and in June of 1980 (upon returning to the states), preached his 1st sermon at his fathers church in Cleveland, Ohio (Christ Temple Missionary Baptist Church).

In 1984, after graduating from the military amphibious warfare school in Quantico, Va. He was transferred to Marine Corps Air Ground Combat Center, in Twentynine Palms, CA. In 1985, he became part time Pastor of Faith In The Word Christian Center, and in 1989 became it's full-time pastor. Over the past 50 years combined of serving both the military and the church, Kevin experienced many opportunities to have Faith to Obey God, in both his personal and professional decision making, and trust God for the ultimate results.

Kevin was born in Cleveland, Ohio but after graduating Ashland University (1976), and receiving his officer commission as a Second Lieutenant, he departed the "cold" Ohio area, and has spent most of his life in the deserts of Twentynine Palms, Ca since the mid 1980s.

Kevin married Malisha L. Long also of Cleveland, Ohio in 1975, and two sons were born to their union. Julian (Tanjier & Kagan), and Jermaine (Tamika & Chase).

Reference

1. [The Open Bible, copyright 1975, Thomas Nelson Inc., Publishers, Nashville, Tennessee, pg. 791, Daniel Chapter 6, written ch. 538 B.C.]

2. H6083 - `aphar - Strong's Hebrew Lexicon (KJV). Retrieved from https://www.blueletterbible.org//lang/lexicon/lexicon.cfm?Strongs=h6083&t=kjv

3. Dake's Annotated Reference Bible, The Old and New Testaments with notes, Concordance and Index, Copyright 1963, by Finis Jennings Dakes, page 737, "Isaiah a sign (20:2)."

Index

A

Aaron, 38, 74, 87–91
Abe, 10
Abed, 80–82
Abednego, 79–81
Abelmeholah, 28
abomination, 103
Abraham, 2–3, 9–15, 31, 36–39, 69–71
accountability, 60
Adam, 58–60, 94, 103, 108, 116
Agag, 56
Ahaz, 106
Amalekites, 27, 55–56, 58
Amitai, 19
Ammon, 15
Amoz, 105–6
angelic dreams, 109, 111
angels, 14, 33, 63, 65–67, 76–77, 85, 110–11, 116–17
anger, 21, 74, 78
apostles, 33, 39, 44, 92
Arimathaea, 52
armour, 62–63
Asher, 28

assignment, 19–20, 31–37, 39, 41, 54, 77, 131
Assyria, 106
authority, 59
Azariah, 79, 82

B

Babylon, 80–82, 84
battle, 26, 29, 117
believer, 7–8, 62–64, 66, 68, 71–72
Belshazzar, 82
Belteshazzar, 79
Bethbarah, 28
Bethel, 47
Bethlehemite, 57
Bethshittah, 28
blood, 62, 65–66, 77, 97
brethren, 15–16, 41, 53, 57, 90, 97, 103

C

Caleb, 38–39
calvary, 35, 44, 117
Chaldeans, 80–82
Chaldees, 11
church, 2, 41, 69, 71, 97, 107, 132
commandments, 52, 55–56, 63, 90
congregation, 39, 87–88, 90–91, 100
creator, 23, 44, 83, 114, 116, 120

D

Damascus, 12, 45
Daniel, 63–64, 79–86, 127
darkness, 8, 62
David, 57, 107, 110–13
decree, 81, 83–84, 86
devil, 34, 62, 103, 117
Diblaim, 108
disciples, 4–6, 8, 16, 44, 76–77, 92
dominion, 68, 71, 86, 117
doors, 18, 34

E

Egypt, 29–30, 35–38, 42, 55, 90, 106
Egyptians, 37
Eleazar, 90
Elijah, 45–50
Elisha, 45, 47–50, 65
Ephraim, 28
Eve, 58–60, 94–95, 100, 103, 116
evil, 21, 58–60, 64, 72, 78, 98, 112, 117
eyes, 16, 24, 43, 54, 65, 68, 72, 87, 98, 100–102, 104, 112

F

faith, 2–7, 10, 29–31, 45–46, 53–55, 60–61, 63, 67–69, 71–72, 74–75, 82, 98–99, 109–10, 125, 130
fight, 25–26, 29, 55, 63–64, 67

flesh, 62, 68, 93–94, 96–98, 101, 103–4, 106, 113
forgiveness, 60, 122, 129
fruit, 58–60, 100, 108, 123

G

Galilee, 52–53, 110
gates, 76, 80
Gideon, 23–31
Gilgal, 47, 56
Gomer, 108
grace, 41–42, 122

H

Hananiah, 79, 82
happiness, 123, 126
Haran, 3, 9, 11, 15
Hearing God, 18–19, 35
heart, 24, 57–58, 71, 74, 98–99, 103, 107, 113
heaven, 10, 16, 30, 34, 47–48, 53, 57, 60, 64, 66–67, 82–83, 86, 100, 112, 116–17
helper, 59
Hezekiah, 105
Holy Ghost, 110–11
Holy Spirit, 73, 75, 99, 103, 125
Hosea, 108

I

idolatry, 56–57
image, 9–10, 34, 79–80, 116
iniquity, 14, 18, 39, 56–57
Isaac, 3, 70
Isaiah, 30, 60, 94, 100, 104–7, 111–12
Israel, 15, 18, 23–24, 27–30, 35–38, 45–46, 55, 57, 70, 87–88, 90, 112–13

J

Jacob, 37–39, 70, 75, 110
jealous, 45–46
Jehovah, 49
Jehu, 45
Jephunneh, 39
Jeremiah, 121, 124
Jericho, 47
Jerusalem, 85, 105
Jesse, 57
Jesus, 4–6, 8, 23, 33, 35, 52–53, 76–77, 92, 101–4, 109, 115–17, 123, 125
Jews, 52, 80–81
Joash, 27
John, 23, 46, 68, 77, 93, 104, 122, 124
Jonah, 19–22, 31, 74–75, 78–79
Joppa, 19
Jordan, 28, 47, 49, 70
Joseph, 37–39, 41–43, 110–11
Joshua, 39, 70–71, 91
Judas, 92

judgement, 87, 94

K

kingdom, 34, 44, 52, 64, 77, 83, 86, 97, 100, 102, 110, 113, 128
knowledge, 58, 60, 68

L

Lebanon, 70
levels, 4, 8, 30–31, 51, 94, 97, 112, 114–15
Lord, 3, 11–14, 16–23, 25–28, 33–34, 36–39, 42–43, 45–47, 53, 55–58, 69–70, 74–75, 97–98, 105–8, 110–12
love, 46, 67–68, 104, 109, 122, 126
Luke, 35, 51–52, 76, 104, 110–11, 131
lust, 101, 104

M

Manasseh, 23, 28
mantle, 46–49
Mark, 122, 124–25, 131
Mary, 52, 109–11
Matthew, 4, 8, 15, 34, 77, 83, 101–2, 111, 113, 116
Midian, 27, 30, 91
Midianites, 23, 25–28
Miriam, 88–89
Mishael, 79, 82
Moabites, 15, 50

Moses, 29–31, 35–39, 70–71, 74, 78, 86–91, 128

N

Nahor, 11
Naphtali, 28
Nathan, 112–13
nations, 36–37, 81, 86, 100, 117
Nebuchadnezzar, King, 80–81
Nineveh, 19–20
Noah, 57

O

obedience, 3, 9, 31, 48, 54, 56, 58, 89, 92, 94, 103, 108, 110, 120, 125
offense, 123, 129
oil, 57

P

peace, 47, 86
Persians, 84, 86
Peter, 5–6
Pharaoh, 29, 42–43, 88, 91
position, 62–64, 66–71, 95
Potiphar, 42
power, 14, 46, 53, 59, 62, 68, 71, 83, 86, 95–96, 110, 122
praise, 76, 129
prayers, 2, 66, 68–69, 84, 124

praying, 81, 84
pride, 103–4, 123
principalities, 62, 68, 71
prisoners, 42, 100
promises, 39, 45, 69, 127
prophets, 19, 45, 47, 75, 104–5, 108

R

Ramah, 57
Rameses, 38
rebellion, 56–57, 103
reconciliation, 115
relationship, 8, 12, 85, 97, 114, 126, 130
Repentance, 124
restoration process, 115
resurrection, 53
righteousness, 63, 67, 77, 113, 115
rock, 46, 87–88, 90–91

S

sacrifice, 18, 49, 56, 58
Saducees, 33
salvation, 49, 64
Samson, 129
Samuel, 16–18, 31, 54–58, 107, 112
Sarai, 9–10
Satan, 95, 97, 102, 117
Saul, 54–58, 112

serpent, 70, 95–96
servants, 12, 27, 43, 65, 70, 106–8
Shadrach, 79, 81
Sodom, 12–13
Solomon, 94
souls, 8, 37–38
stubbornness, 56–57
submission, 59, 103
success, 3, 6, 34, 37
Succoth, 38
Supernatural, 111, 118
Syria, 45

T

temple, 16, 33–34, 102, 105
temptation, 76, 104
Terah, 11
test, 3, 8, 74, 82, 84, 101–4
timing, 35–37, 39, 115–16
Timothy, 40, 46, 67, 115
trumpets, 27–28, 66–67, 98
trust, 72, 98–99, 112, 115, 126, 129

U

understanding, 68, 72, 89, 94, 98–99, 104, 110, 112, 118–19
UNITY, 125
Uzziah, King, 105

V

victory, 26, 45–46, 63, 67, 71–72
vision, 18, 64, 82, 109
voice, 7–11, 15–19, 21–23, 25–26, 28–32, 35, 42, 46, 53, 55–56, 63, 66–67, 91, 130

W

whirlwind, 47–48, 50
wilderness, 30, 38–39, 45, 70, 100–102, 104
wisdom, 22, 31, 44, 68, 98
wormwood, 66–67
worship, 80–81, 93, 102

Z

Zeeb, 28
Zererath, 28

www.ingramcontent.com/pod-product-compliance
Lightning Source LLC
Chambersburg PA
CBHW071735080526
44588CB00013B/2036